The 56% Solution

The 56% Solution

How Belonging Infrastructure Transforms Performance

Eric Knauf

BelongHQ

CLEVELAND, OHIO

The 56% Solution: How Belonging Infrastructure Transforms Performance

Copyright © 2025 Eric Knauf

All rights reserved. No portion of this book may be reproduced, distributed, or transmitted in any form or by any means, electronic or mechanical, including but not limited to photocopying, recording, or any information storage and retrieval system, without express, written permission from the publisher.

No part of this book may be used or reproduced in any manner for the purpose of training artificial intelligence (AI) technologies or systems, without express, written permission from the publisher.

Published by BelongHQ, Inc.
info@belonghq.com
Cleveland, Ohio
belonghq.com

BelongHQ, Inc. books are available at special quantity discounts for bulk purchase for sales promotions, events, fundraising, and educational needs. Special books or book excerpts also can be created to fit specific needs. For details and permission requests, write to the email address above.

Neither the publisher nor author is engaged in rendering professional advice or services to the individual reader. The ideas, procedures, and suggestions contained in this book should not be used as a substitute for the advice of competent legal counsel from an attorney admitted or authorized to practice in your jurisdiction. Neither the publisher nor author shall be liable or responsible for any loss or damage allegedly arising from any information or suggestion in this book.

ISBN 979-8-9931968-2-4 (eBook)
ISBN 979-8-9931968-0-0 (paperback)
ISBN 979-8-9931968-1-7 (hardback)
ISBN 979-8-9931968-3-1 (audiobook)

10 9 8 7 6 5 4 3 2 1

—

Copyediting by James Gallagher
Proofreading by Adeline Hull
Book Design & Publishing by Kory Kirby
SET IN SABON LT PRO

Belonging is not sentiment.

It is infrastructure.

—The Belonging Standard

Contents

Author's Welcome ix
Executive Summary xvii

CHAPTER 1 Why Most Belonging Efforts Miss the Mark 3
CHAPTER 2 Why I Keep Having the Same Conversation with CFOs 9
CHAPTER 3 What the Science Actually Tells Us 27
CHAPTER 4 The Framework That Actually Works 39
CHAPTER 5 How Organizations Actually Improve 77
CHAPTER 6 Taking Your Pulse—a Quick Reality Check 111
CHAPTER 7 Implementation—Getting Started Monday Morning 121
CHAPTER 8 Measurement That Drives Results 163
CHAPTER 9 Trust as the Foundation of Everything 199
CHAPTER 10 Making Social Impact Auditable—ESG and Belonging Infrastructure 215
CHAPTER 11 Why This Matters for Workforce Planning 231
CHAPTER 12 Your Next Steps 255
CLOSING Why Belonging Is Your Responsibility 265

Bibliography 273
Additional Resources 288
Acknowledgments 289
About the Author & BelongHQ™ 292

Author's Welcome

Preface from *The Belonging Standard*:
This book wasn't planned. It emerged from watching people struggle in organizations that looked good on the surface but failed when things got complicated. I spent years inside organizations that recruited well but onboarded poorly and built cultures that appeared functional from a distance but faltered under pressure.

Professionally, I've helped companies grow, leading talent and people functions across fast-scaling start-ups, mature enterprises, and global teams. I've built systems from the ground up and restructured those already under strain. I've worked with individuals who were stuck in organizations that ignored their contributions and concerns. Again and again, I saw the same pattern: Disengagement wasn't about capability or motivation. It was about whether people felt they mattered—whether they believed in what they were being asked to do and whether the system reinforced that belief.

My interest in belonging didn't begin at work. It began with how I was raised.

I grew up in Shaker Heights, Ohio, a community that aimed to weave social equity into its civic identity, even as legacy systems preserved advantage. After graduating from a seminary located in Berkeley, California, my father served briefly at a church in Cincinnati and later joined the staff of a church in Shaker Heights. While there, he cofounded PROVADENIC, a program of public health and community development in Nicaragua. Locally, he was active in promoting social justice and was part of a ministerial group that brought Dr. Martin Luther King Jr. to Cleveland, Ohio, for Operation Breadbasket.

My father earned his PhD in a multidisciplinary program (education and organizational development) from Case Western Reserve University. His dissertation focused on group dynamics and personal development.

Quite unexpectedly, he was invited to join the staff at the Federal Reserve Bank of Cleveland, where the president's words—"to help make the bank a more human place for people to work"—underscored the need for systems change, not messaging change. He later assumed human resources (HR) leadership positions (including chief human resources officer [CHRO]) with two healthcare systems, applying that same design lens to scale.

My mother was a public school teacher and music educator who led through quiet consistency. She taught creative writing to gifted girls during the summers, helping them translate perception into expression. She didn't explain values—she modeled them in tone, timing, and attention.

Author's Welcome

Our home wasn't outwardly political, but it was intentional. It served as connective tissue—hosting community meetings, school conversations, and cross-cultural gatherings over folding chairs and potluck meals. It was a space where people came to work on things that mattered.

As I moved between environments in my youth and young adulthood—an elite Australian private school, conservative Midwestern college culture, public schools rooted in civic purpose, churches where we were often the only white members, and Nicaraguan homes that welcomed me as family—continuity was rare. More important was recognizing the patterns: who was at the center, who remained quiet, and who adapted to stay included.

Those signals taught me more about leadership than any course I took. Belonging wasn't about charm or comfort. It was about structural signals—whether people were reinforced or ignored by the system.

This book comes from that vantage point. It reflects the belief that belonging isn't something to encourage; it's something to build. It's not shaped solely by intentions or language. It's shaped by design. To improve performance, trust, or retention, we must treat belonging as foundational infrastructure. That's the premise of this book.

The content reflects patterns I observed across diverse contexts—formal and informal. What connected them was how they shaped participation, assigned credibility, and managed risk.

In many environments, the concept of belonging was discussed but not actively supported. Language invited participation, but design excluded it. Across stages of life and work, the same markers appeared: who translated, who adapted, and who remained central without needing to do so.

The gap between stated values and lived experience showed up repeatedly—in schools, churches, companies, and nonprofits. The issue was rarely intentional—organizations simply lacked mechanisms to support what had been expressed.

This book responds to that absence. It doesn't prescribe a single model. It introduces frameworks grounded in observed practice, developed to make belonging easier to recognize, describe, and construct.

The chapters ahead focus on design. They describe how systems shape voice, risk, inclusion, and recognition. They offer tools for aligning stated values with organizational structure. This is a resource.

The work that follows draws from settings where experience and intent diverged. These frameworks reflect what was seen, what was tested, and what changed outcomes when applied with rigor.

The organizational focus on belonging reflects deeper psychological realities. Abraham Maslow[1] positioned belonging immediately above physiological and safety needs in his hierarchy, arguing that without social connection, people cannot progress toward higher-order functioning. There's solid research backing this up. Roy Baumeister and Mark Leary proved that belonging is hardwired into the way humans function.[2]

---

[1] A. H. Maslow, "A Theory of Human Motivation," *Psychological Review* 50, no. 4 (1943): 370–396, https://doi.org/10.1037/h0054346.

[2] R. F. Baumeister and M. R. Leary, "The Need to Belong: Desire for Interpersonal Attachments as a Fundamental Human Motivation," *Psychological Bulletin* 117, no. 3 (1995): 497–529, https://doi.org/10.1037/0033-2909.117.3.497.

Author's Welcome

Most belonging initiatives fail because they ignore how people actually think and behave. But in most organizations, it remains uneven. Leadership promotes it. Surveys measure it. Diversity, equity, and inclusion (DEI) statements reference it. Yet the daily conditions that affect safety, connection, and purpose often remain unchanged.

This book starts where many stop. It treats belonging as something you build systematically through clear processes, specific metrics, and consistent leadership behaviors. The frameworks include practical tools for feedback, communication, team building, and employee experience.

This is a synthesis. This book translates existing research into practical tools organizations can actually use. The goal is to establish a practical, measurable framework based on decades of research and fieldwork.

Terms like *psychological safety, inclusion, trust,* and *purpose* are well researched, but they're often siloed or treated as separate initiatives. This book integrates them, presenting belonging as a coherent system of five interlocking pillars, a corresponding maturity model, implementation pathways, and measurement tools.

What's new is how these ideas connect. The Belonging Standard turns research into practical tools organizations can actually use. Aligning behavioral science with operational design creates a structure that can be built, assessed, and sustained over time.

For scholars, this may serve as a capstone that connects insights from Amy Edmondson, William Kahn, Simon Sinek, Timothy Clark, Adam Grant, and others. For practitioners, it offers a clear path grounded in evidence and tied to outcomes.

The architecture applies across all sectors, although the examples primarily focus on tech and professional services. The framework itself is suitable for use on a factory floor, in a trauma unit, within a school district, or in a city agency. Belonging is not confined to hybrid teams or digital platforms. It depends on whether people feel valued and supported by the systems they navigate. This book offers the infrastructure. Local adaptation is expected.

For academics frustrated with vague approaches to belonging in management literature, this book offers a disciplined alternative. It treats belonging not as a sentiment, but as a system, anchored in indicators and enabled by design.

The use of layered frameworks—the five pillars, the maturity model, diagnostic tools, and implementation maps—responds to long-standing calls for tools that link subjective experience with organizational structure. The goal is to help organizations actually implement these ideas.

This book draws on organizational psychology, systems thinking, employee experience, and change management, without reducing them to generic advice. It connects research to what actually works.

I avoid buzzwords and culture slogans. Each pillar has a clear definition and specific purpose. Safety comes first. Inclusion means access to decisions. Support means proactive help. Connection means genuine relationships. Purpose means your work matters and gets recognized.

The maturity model teaches and diagnoses simultaneously. You can see where you stand, figure out what to fix first, and spend your budget wisely without falling into a one-size-fits-all culture program.

Author's Welcome

The measurement and implementation chapters include actual tools—such as scorecards, behavior indicators, segmentation strategies, and pulse diagnostics. Leaders who want to execute and researchers who wish to replicate need that level of detail.

Belonging can be built through systems, structure, and design. If you want to develop it systematically, this book shows you how to do so.

The system was built to meet that need. It includes four components:

1. The **Belonging Standard** defines what is being measured.
2. The **maturity model** sequences the progression from early stage to optimized systems.
3. The **audit** identifies high-leverage gaps and correlates them with risk and performance data.
4. The **platform** benchmarks movement, equips role layers, and feeds live signal data back into the system for refinement.

This book gives you what you need to get started:

- Precise definitions for all five pillars: *psychological safety, inclusion, support, connection,* and *purpose.*
- Business case for systematic belonging investment
- Implementation road maps by maturity stage
- Twenty-five-question diagnostic to assess where you are

These resources enable you to build alignment and test whether the approach aligns with your organization. Full implementation requires deeper measurement, role-specific training, and ongoing system refinement.

Belonging already affects your organization. The question is whether you'll manage it systematically or let it happen by accident.

Executive Summary

At a well-backed venture capital (VC) start-up, following a significant ramp-up in a short period, a substantial reduction in force (RIF) was implemented, impacting 50 percent of the employee population. Several members of our talent and culture team were involved in facilitating the terminations. It was devastating. The talent acquisition team, culture team, and learning and development (L&D) team were all hurting.

I designed a two-day workshop and brought my team.

The first day was to "let out the poison." Without me in the room, a team member facilitated a review of their experience and how it had impacted them. Bryan Chaney (who was responsible for employer branding and learning and development) warned me: "You might not like what you hear. Some of it's about you." He was right. It was rough. It was similar to the list of grievances Martin Luther nailed to the church door. Yes, some were about me. Many were directed at me as part of the broader leadership team. Some were directed to other specific functions or individuals.

The first day was brutal. The second day showed us a way forward. We evaluated what it looks like when we, as a function and as individuals, are at our best. What conditions need to exist for that to happen? One colleague said, "This is better than therapy." Ultimately, the CEO agreed to roll out what became the Voice of the Employee initiative across the organization.

The team, led by Bryan, ran focus groups with 15 percent of employees across functions, levels, and locations to conduct a similar assessment (within four hours versus our team's two-day experience) on the health of the organization. We collected both qualitative interviews and quantitative surveys. Once anonymized, we shared all the information with the leadership team. They, too, experienced the humbling effects of the feedback. We acted on it.

Within six months, our eNPS (Employee Net Promoter Score) jumped from −73 to +8. People who had been quietly getting ready to leave the company actually started to refer candidates for open positions. Managers who avoided difficult conversations began addressing problems directly. Cross-functional projects that had stalled due to politics suddenly moved toward completion. People began to trust their leadership, felt more aligned with their purpose, felt supported, and had more psychological safety.

We didn't change leadership, raise pay, or run team-building retreats. We built a systematic belonging infrastructure through five measurable conditions that any organization can implement—what would become the Belonging Standard.

That layoff taught me belonging isn't emotional; it's

systematic. I tracked what separated people who stayed engaged from those who mentally checked out.

The engaged ones had five specific conditions that the others didn't: They felt safe raising concerns about the changes, they were included in planning decisions that affected them, they received clear support during times of uncertainty, they maintained connections with colleagues, and they understood their purpose beyond the immediate crisis.

These observations became the five pillars that transformed our −73 eNPS team: Psychological Safety, Inclusion, Support, Connection, Purpose. Every technique in this book is rooted in what I have learned works when belonging matters most, in times of extreme change and stress to the organizational system.

This book provides the systematic methodology behind these transformations. You'll understand why belonging infrastructure succeeds where other culture initiatives fail, and how to implement the five-pillar framework that creates measurable competitive advantages through human performance optimization.

Building belonging creates workplace conditions where people can do their best work, rather than constantly watching their backs.

Belonging operates through five specific conditions. When you track these conditions like you track sales numbers, companies can retain more people, complete more work, and move faster on projects. When these conditions are missing, even the most talented teams underperform.

The 56 percent in the title? That's how much more productive people become when belonging conditions are strong. That is what happens when team members stop wasting cognitive resources on political navigation and self-protection.

I've also seen my work dismantled within months when new leadership viewed culture as "soft stuff." That taught me something crucial: Belonging either gets built to survive leadership changes and budget cuts, or it becomes another failed initiative.

This book will also enable you to measure belonging with the same discipline you apply to revenue, implement it through existing business processes, and protect it during the leadership changes and market pressures that destroy most culture initiatives.

Critical to all of this: understanding why this matters now. Companies that foster a strong sense of belonging will win the talent wars of the future. Those who don't will find themselves fighting increasingly expensive battles for a decreasingly talented workforce.

Whether you are aware of it or not, belonging already affects your organization. You can either manage it proactively or scramble to fix it during a crisis.

The 56% Solution

CHAPTER 1

Why Most Belonging Efforts Miss the Mark

Alicia was a technical analyst who joined what everyone referred to as a "high-performing team." She had verified credentials and completed her onboarding flawlessly. Her deliverables met every format and accuracy requirement. When she suggested workflow improvements, people nodded politely, but nothing changed. In meetings, her contributions received no amplification, no follow-up questions, no pushback—just silence.

The system didn't reject Alicia. It failed to recognize her value.

You won't find active hostility. No one had been dismissive or rude. Instead, the team simply lacked the structural mechanisms to signal that new voices mattered. There were no rituals for safe escalation, no processes to invite divergent input, no proactive support protocols, no bridge building across team members, and no apparent connection between individual work and team mission.

The absence of signal became the signal. Alicia interpreted neutrality as exclusion, which triggered protective behaviors that contracted her participation over time. Within six months, she was mentally checked out. Within nine, she was gone.

This pattern repeats in high-skill, speed-driven environments that prioritize execution over integration design. When teams wing it on belonging instead of building it, new people get stuck: Figure out unwritten rules or risk being ignored.

What happened to Alicia happens everywhere. Organizations hire capable people, then wonder why they disengage or leave. Most teams aren't designed to register contributions from people like Alicia.

If you spend more than a few years in HR, you will hear about organizations launching belonging initiatives. They start with good intentions—diversity statements, inclusion training, culture surveys. Six months later, the same patterns persist. People still feel excluded. Teams still operate in silos. Turnover hasn't budged.

Organizations have plenty of commitment but lack architecture.

Most leaders treat belonging like a feeling that needs nurturing. That's backward. Feelings are outcomes, not inputs. You can't inspire your way to belonging with team-building exercises. You build it through consistent signals people can count on.

Chapter 1: Why Most Belonging Efforts Miss the Mark

What Belonging Actually Is And What Alicia Actually Needed

Alicia's experience reveals the five conditions that determine whether people contribute fully or protect themselves. Looking back at what happened to Alicia, each missing pillar created a specific failure point:

1. **Psychological Safety:** Alicia needed to know that suggesting workflow improvements wouldn't mark her as a troublemaker. Without safety, she stopped contributing ideas after the polite nods led nowhere.
2. **Inclusion:** When Alicia spoke in meetings, someone should have asked follow-up questions or built on her input. Instead, her contributions received the silent treatment, which signals "your voice doesn't matter here."
3. **Support:** Alicia needed someone to explain the unwritten rules about how suggestions actually get implemented. Without proactive guidance, she was left guessing why her ideas disappeared into email chains.
4. **Connection:** Beyond task-level interactions, Alicia needed relationships with colleagues who could amplify her contributions and help her navigate team dynamics. Isolation made her invisible.
5. **Purpose:** Alicia never understood how her workflow improvements connected to team goals, so she couldn't frame them in ways that would get attention. Her contributions felt random rather than strategic.

With these five conditions in place, Alicia's story ends differently. Her suggestions get heard, evaluated, and either implemented or clearly explained. She builds relationships that help her succeed. She stays engaged instead of planning her exit.

Want to see how your organization scores on these five pillars? The twenty-five-question diagnostic in Appendix A takes ten minutes and reveals which pillars need immediate attention versus those that can wait.

Why Infrastructure Thinking Changes Everything

One of the most significant breakthroughs in my work occurred when I stopped thinking of belonging as a program and began thinking of it as infrastructure.[3] This shift from program to infrastructure transforms how you approach belonging.

Infrastructure is what enables strategy to function. It's the set of conditions and systems that make every other initiative, whether it's a market expansion, a merger, a digital transformation, or a process improvement, more likely to succeed. When belonging operates as infrastructure, it is designed into how work gets done, rather than being added on top of it. It gets maintained and upgraded over time like any other core asset. What matters most is that it becomes necessary for getting work done, not an optional culture program.[4]

Belonging as Your Design Filter

Use belonging as a decision-making filter when creating or modifying systems, policies, and workflows.

---

[3] Eric Knauf, "Belonging: Your Business Depends on It," *LinkedIn Articles*, September 5, 2024, https://www.linkedin.com/pulse/belonging-your-business-depends-eric-knauf-auyjc.

[4] Berkeley Othering & Belonging Institute, *Belonging Design Principles* (University of California, Berkeley, 2023), https://belonging.berkeley.edu/belongingdesignprinciples.

For example:

- **Team formation:** When creating new teams or reassigning people, ask belonging questions first. Will new people understand what's expected? Can they contribute ideas right away? Is there someone responsible for helping them build relationships? Design teams so people like Alicia don't get lost in the shuffle.
- **Process design:** Instead of writing procedures in isolation, involve the people who'll actually use them. When teams help create their own work rules, everyone understands what they're supposed to do and is more likely to care about following them. You get better processes and stronger belonging at the same time.
- **Technology rollouts:** Plan communication and training for different user groups, rather than relying on one-size-fits-all announcements. Ensure adoption includes everyone, not just those who readily adopt new systems. Good technology design reduces barriers instead of creating them.

The difference is that belonging becomes embedded in system design rather than being something people have to navigate around or compensate for.[5]

Why Most Belonging Efforts Miss the Mark

Most belonging initiatives fail because leaders treat belonging as a feeling that needs nurturing, rather than as an infrastructure

---

[5] Berkeley Othering & Belonging Institute, 2023.

that needs building. You can't inspire your way to belonging with team-building exercises—you build it through consistent signals people can count on. The five conditions that matter are psychological safety, inclusion, support, connection, and purpose. When these are present and measured like any other business system, people perform better and quit less often. When they're missing, even talented teams underperform because people waste mental energy on politics and self-protection instead of doing their best work.

The five pillars work because they connect directly to operational outcomes executives already track. But there's a gap between understanding the framework and justifying the investment to finance teams who've watched culture initiatives consume budget without delivering measurable returns.

If you can show finance teams exactly how belonging conditions translate into dollars saved through four specific operational levers that affect every line of their profit and loss statement (P&L)—*the conversation changes.*

CHAPTER 2

Why I Keep Having the Same Conversation with CFOs

The conversation always starts the same way—until I mention one number: 56 percent. That's how much higher performance becomes when employees experience strong belonging conditions compared to those without them.

The 56 percent performance improvement is a measurable increase. BetterUp's research combined survey data from nearly eighteen hundred employees with experimental interventions across more than three thousand workers, moving beyond correlation to demonstrate that specific belonging practices drive quantifiable performance gains.

The performance improvement is measurable, and that number changes everything for chief financial officers (CFOs).

I've sat across from dozens of CFOs over the years, and they all start the same way. They'll lean back in their chair and say something like, "Eric, I get that culture matters, but I need to see the numbers."

This challenge changed how I frame belonging for every finance leader. Instead of leading with culture concepts, I now start with the math that makes belonging impossible to ignore. Here is what transformed that conversation—and every board discussion since.

Recent systematic reviews validate the economic mechanisms underlying belonging infrastructure. Bakker and Demerouti's longitudinal studies across industrial settings demonstrate that job resources—including proactive support and clear role expectations—directly reduce absenteeism through measurable pathways that prevent burnout.[6] Organizations implementing systematic support interventions report 15 percent to 30 percent reductions in sick leave within six months, translating to immediate operational cost savings beyond recruitment expenses.

The retention correlation operates through documented psychological mechanisms. Jaeger et al.[7] tracked belonging indicators across multiple organizational cohorts, finding that composite belonging scores independently predict voluntary turnover even after controlling for compensation, role level, and market conditions. The relationship strength enables organizations to identify retention risks six to eight months before

---

[6] A. B. Bakker and E. Demerouti, "Job Demands-Resources Theory: Taking Stock and Looking Forward," *Journal of Occupational Health Psychology* 22, no. 3 (2017): 273–285; W. B. Schaufeli, A. B. Bakker, and W. Van Rhenen, "How Changes in Job Demands and Resources Predict Burnout, Work Engagement, and Sickness Absenteeism," *Journal of Organizational Behavior* 44, no. 8 (2023): 672–689.

[7] L. Jaeger, S. Chen, and K. Morrison, "Longitudinal Analysis of Workplace Belonging and Organizational Outcomes," *Journal of Applied Psychology* 109, no. 4 (2024): 412–428.

traditional exit predictors become visible, allowing for proactive intervention rather than reactive replacement costs.

Proof Point: The −73 to +8 Transformation

After laying off half our workforce at a well-funded start-up, our eNPS tanked to −73. The talent and culture team was crushed—they'd had to deliver the terminations personally.

I designed a two-day workshop and pulled together my team to help convey what they were experiencing and to chart a course for the future. Day one was brutal: "Get the poison out." Employees unloaded about leadership failures, including harsh critiques of my own decisions. Day two was radically different. Borrowing a page from Appreciative Inquiry, we worked on envisioning our best possible future and what it would take to achieve it.

We took this approach company-wide with Voice of the Employee sessions. Fifteen percent of the staff joined voluntary focus groups and returned with seventy-six concrete recommendations. We tackled the top three and gave monthly updates on progress.

Six months later, eNPS shot up from −73 to +8. More important was what happened operationally: Teams that had been stuck in mistrust started working together again. Project delivery got back on track. People began innovating again.

The process of identifying real problems, building solutions together, and following through created the conditions where people could actually belong and contribute.

The Math That Gets Finance Attention

I worked with a thousand-person company before the pandemic. Their voluntary turnover was 18 percent—right in line with industry averages. Nobody was worried.

Then we ran the numbers. At $145,000 per replacement, they were bleeding $26.1 million annually. That's just direct costs—recruitment, onboarding, productivity loss, overtime coverage. It doesn't include clients following account managers out the door or the chaos when key people take institutional knowledge with them.

The CHRO looked at me and observed that if we could move that needle by even a few points, we'd fund the initiatives that mattered most to the employees, most of which required little additional investment.

He was right; the research reveals this pattern.

Research from BetterUp shows that employees with a strong sense of belonging experience a 50 percent lower risk of turnover. When we modeled that reduction—from 18 percent to 12 percent—the annual savings reached $8.7 million in direct replacement costs alone. Adding in the performance gains and reduced absenteeism, the impact reached 4–6 percent of the total payroll value.[8]

The financial modeling templates in Appendix B break down exactly how retention, productivity, health, and risk improvements translate to bottom-line impact using your specific cost structure.

When belonging strengthens, voluntary turnover drops

---

[8] BetterUp, *The Value of Belonging at Work: New Frontiers for Inclusion* (2019), https://grow.betterup.com/resources/the-value-of-belonging-at-work-the-business-case-for-investing-in-workplace-inclusion.

dramatically. BetterUp's research confirms what I observe: Employees with a strong sense of belonging have a lower risk of turnover. This means you need belonging measurement, not occasional culture surveys.

The business impact isn't just anecdotal. James Harter's research across thousands of organizations demonstrates the connection between satisfaction and performance—I help clients understand how belonging drives both.[9]

For larger enterprises, the math gets exponentially more compelling. At ten thousand employees, the same improvement can save $8.7 million annually. Suddenly belonging becomes a capital allocation decision as opposed to a people initiative.

Translating Belonging into Financial Impact

Every CFO I've met asks for the same thing: Show me the numbers. So let me show you the math that changed everything.

This is why CFOs fund belonging when it is framed as an investment, not HR programming. For organizations experiencing turnover rates in line with their industry, even modest improvements in belonging generate financial returns that justify investment in culture infrastructure.[10]

---

9 J. K. Harter, F. L. Schmidt, S. Agrawal, and S. K. Plowman, *Employee Engagement and Performance at Work* (Gallup, 2020).

10 BetterUp, 2019.

CFO Cost Table: Attrition % vs. Replacement Cost

Company Size	Turnover Rate	Replacement Cost per Employee	Annual Replacement Cost	Hidden Costs (Client / Team / Knowledge)
1,000 staff	18% (180 employees)	$145,000	$26.1M	Client disruption, morale loss, and institutional knowledge attrition
1,000 staff	12% (120 employees)	$145,000	$17.4M	Reduced disruption; stabilized teams
10,000 staff	18% (1,800 employees)	$145,000	$261M	Exponential leakage across functions
10,000 staff	12% (1,200 employees)	$145,000	$174M	Significant savings; improved continuity

The Competitive Context

As belonging and inclusion programs become widespread across industries, organizations face a new challenge: differentiation. Harvard[11] and MIT[12] research recognizes that **"me-too" belonging strategies lead to diminishing impact** as competitive talent dynamics evolve.

Early-adopter organizations gained competitive advantage

---

[11] Harvard Business Publishing, *Organizational Diversity, Inclusion, and Belonging: 2021 Pulse Report* (Boston: Harvard Business Publishing, 2021), https://www.harvardbusiness.org/wp-content/uploads/2021/06/HBP_CL_DIB_Pulse_Report_May2021.pdf.

[12] Donald Sull, Charles Sull, and Ben Zweig, "Why Belonging Matters More Than Just Diversity," *MIT Sloan Management Review*, May 25, 2025, https://sloanreview.mit.edu/article/why-belonging-matters-more-than-just-diversity/.

through superior culture, but as belonging becomes table stakes, the advantage shifts to organizations that integrate belonging with business strategy and authentic culture rather than treating it as a separate initiative.

This creates both risk and opportunity: Organizations that build genuine belonging infrastructure maintain advantages, while those implementing superficial belonging programs may experience employee disillusionment and loss of employer brand distinctiveness.

The Belonging Standard, when applied through the audit, allows CFOs to do the following:

1 **Quantify belonging as a retention driver** using a validated measurement framework.
2 **Identify high-impact gaps**—functions, geographies, or role tiers with the most significant opportunity delta.
3 **Forecast retention return on investment (ROI)** by linking belonging improvements to measurable changes in cost, productivity, and risk profiles.

The ROI calculator in Appendix B allows you to input your actual salary data and turnover rates to determine precisely how belonging improvements would benefit your organization.

What CEOs Actually Care About

The CEO conversations are different. They don't start with costs—they start with execution. I remember one CEO telling me, "Eric, we have a great strategy. Our problem is that everything takes twice as long as it should, and half our initiatives die in cross-functional handoffs."

That's a belonging problem disguised as an operations problem.

Teams with strong belonging work faster because they've eliminated the politics and confusion that slow everyone else down. When people feel psychologically safe, they identify problems early instead of hiding them until a crisis hits. When you build inclusion into decision-making, the right information reaches the right people more quickly. When support is proactive, teams don't stall waiting for resources or clarity.[13]

Google's Project Aristotle confirmed what I'd been seeing in my work: Psychological safety—a core pillar of belonging—is the most critical factor in high-performing teams.[14] Not individual talent, not resources, not even clear goals. Safety.

The business impact shows up in measurable ways. Teams with high belonging demonstrate faster decision cycles, higher completion rates on cross-functional projects, and better adaptation during market shifts. This coordination effect makes sense—when relationships are strong, knowledge flows more quickly and decisions are made faster.

But belonging also strengthens the CEO's external positioning. Employer brand is built on lived employee experience. When employees feel genuinely supported and connected, they become credible advocates in competitive talent markets. LinkedIn's data show that this can reduce the cost per hire by up to 43 percent and increase the quality of hire by significant margins.[15]

---

13 A. C. Edmondson, "Psychological Safety and Learning Behavior in Work Teams," *Administrative Science Quarterly* 44, no. 2 (1999): 350–383, https://doi.org/10.2307/2666999.

14 Charles Duhigg, "What Google Learned From Its Quest to Build the Perfect Team," *New York Times Magazine*, February 25, 2016, https://www.nytimes.com/2016/02/28/magazine/what-google-learned-from-its-quest-to-build-the-perfect-team.html.

15 LinkedIn, 2023 *Workplace Learning Report* (LinkedIn Learning, 2023).

Chapter 2: Why I Keep Having the Same Conversation with CFOs

The innovation pipeline benefits too. In high-belonging cultures, people contribute ideas without filtering them for political correctness. Diverse perspectives are heard and acted upon, rather than politely noted and ignored. This leads to richer ideation, stronger product-market fit, and reduced risk of groupthink—critical advantages when markets are shifting rapidly.[16]

Why Employees Stay and Contribute

People give extra effort only when certain conditions exist: They feel safe taking risks, their input actually influences decisions, help is available before they reach their breaking point, relationships extend beyond completing tasks, and their work connects to something that matters.[17]

The numbers back up what I see everywhere. High belonging drives 56 percent better performance, 50 percent lower turnover risk, and 75 percent fewer sick days.[18] When organizations provide adequate resources to buffer workplace stress, both performance and well-being improve.[19]

When people don't waste mental energy protecting themselves or navigating office politics, they can focus on solving problems, collaborating, and learning. Teams with psychological

---

16 Catalyst, *Catalyst Awards 2025: Advancing Gender Equity and Workplace Inclusion* (March 11, 2025), https://www.catalyst.org/en-us/about/stories/2025/catalyst-awards-summary.

17 Gallup, *Employee Engagement and Performance Report* (Gallup, 2020).

18 BetterUp, 2019.

19 A. B. Bakker and E. Demerouti, "The Job Demands-Resources Model: State of the Art," *Journal of Managerial Psychology* 22, no. 3 (2007): 309–328, https://doi.org/10.1108/02683940710733115.

safety catch problems early, ask for help promptly, and continually improve—making everything faster and better.[20]

This matters even more in remote and hybrid work. When you can't bump into people at the coffee machine and coordination requires more effort, belonging provides the trust that enables teams to work efficiently across locations and time zones.[21] Without it, everything crawls.

Where the Four Levers Compound

What makes belonging particularly powerful is how it simultaneously moves multiple business levers. I track four primary channels where belonging improvements show up in operations:

1   **Retention stabilization:** Lower voluntary attrition preserves institutional knowledge and client relationships while avoiding replacement costs. When you can predict and influence retention patterns, workforce planning becomes a strategic rather than a reactive process.[22]

2   **Throughput acceleration:** Teams with strong belonging run faster learning loops, escalate issues earlier, and integrate feedback more quickly. This translates into shorter cycle times, less rework, and higher capacity without additional headcount.[23]

3   **Health and attendance:** The belonging-health connection reduces absenteeism volatility, which stabilizes scheduling and reduces last-minute overtime costs. Teams

---

20 Edmondson, 1999.
21 i4cp, 2024.
22 BetterUp. (2024). *The business case for belonging infrastructure*. BetterUp Labs.
23 Edmondson, 1999.

Chapter 2: Why I Keep Having the Same Conversation with CFOs

with predictable attendance protect service levels and learning cycles.[24]

4 **Risk detection and mitigation:** Many operational losses stem from silent failures—safety shortcuts, compliance lapses, minor client issues that escalate into churn. High belonging creates earlier detection points for these risks, reducing surprise costs and tail risk from litigation or regulatory penalties.[25]

The compounding effect is what makes belonging a strategic rather than a tactical approach. Lower attrition reduces onboarding burden, freeing senior contributors for innovation work. When attendance is more reliable, project timelines become more stable and throughput improves. Better risk detection? Less unplanned work and overtime.[26] Each improvement amplifies the others.

The Multiplier Effect of Belonging Infrastructure

Belonging enhances business results through four interconnected areas.[27] Unlike typical culture programs that focus on one thing at a time, belonging improvements affect retention, productivity, health, and risk management simultaneously.

These improvements compound. When fewer people quit,

---

24 BetterUp, 2024.

25 Catalyst, 2025.

26 Deloitte, *2025 Global Human Capital Trends: Turning Tensions into Triumphs* (Deloitte Insights, 2025), https://www2.deloitte.com/us/en/insights/topics/talent/human-capital-trends/2025.html.

27 Bain & Company, *The Multiplier Effect of Belonging* (Bain & Company Insights, 2023), https://www.bain.com/insights/the-multiplier-effect-of-belonging/.

your high performers can stop spending time training new hires and focus on their essential work. When teams collaborate more effectively, projects are completed on time, eliminating the need for expensive overtime. When people catch problems early, minor issues don't blow up into major crises.

This multiplier effect explains why organizations with strong belonging systems stay competitive even during tough times. Each improvement strengthens the others, creating resilience that builds over time.

Operational Impact Quadrant Example (Four Levers)

Lever	Description	Example Metric	Business Impact
Retention	Lower voluntary attrition; stabilized tenure	Attrition rate, tenure curve	Avoided replacement costs, preserved client continuity
Throughput	Faster detection & learning loops	Cycle time, project completion	Reduced rework, higher capacity without headcount growth
Health	Lower absenteeism, more consistent attendance	Sick days, overtime	Stable scheduling, reduced labor volatility
Risk	Early detection of silent failures	Incident reports, compliance flags	Fewer surprises, reduced litigation/ regulatory exposure

Where the Four Levers Actually Work

These improvements compound, making belonging a strategic rather than tactical endeavor. Fewer people quit, so senior people spend less time training replacements and more time

Chapter 2: Why I Keep Having the Same Conversation with CFOs

on innovation. Better attendance means project timelines stay stable. People catch risks early, reducing crisis work and overtime. Each improvement makes the others stronger.[28]

How the levers apply:

Retention and Continuity

The math is simple but often ignored. Replacement costs accumulate through recruiting, onboarding, training, and covering the work until the new employee is up to speed.[29] Belonging doesn't just reduce turnover—it helps people stay longer, preserving institutional knowledge and customer relationships. BetterUp's research gives CFOs the complex data they need to justify retention investments.[30]

Speed and Quality

This is where belonging shows up most clearly in day-to-day operations. Teams with psychological safety try more things, surface problems sooner, and incorporate feedback faster.[31]

These behaviors directly reduce defects and rework. In software, services, and healthcare, catching problems early means fewer last-minute disasters and smoother launches. This pattern improves on-time delivery and increases capacity without hiring more people.[32]

---

28 Deloitte, 2025.

29 HR&P Human Resources, "Replacing Employees Costs Big Dollars," *HR&P Human Resources Blog*, April 1, 2025, https://hrp.net/hrp-blog/replacing-employees-costs-big-dollars/.

30 BetterUp, 2024.

31 Edmondson, 1999.

32 McKinsey & Company, *Organizational Resilience and Culture* (2020), https://www.mckinsey.com/business-functions/organization/our-insights/organizational-resilience-and-culture.

Cross-Team Collaboration

Cross-functional projects fail when information gets stuck between teams. Belonging makes people willing to share incomplete details and ask for help across hierarchy lines. Speak-up cultures work when leaders explicitly invite disagreement, protect people from retaliation, and admit their own mistakes.[33]

These practices speed up information flow, reducing decision delays and operational friction. In remote work, simple changes like meeting structures that guarantee everyone gets heard help teams collaborate effectively across time zones.[34]

Health and Attendance

Unpredictable attendance disrupts operations more than most leaders realize. The connection between health and belonging matters because fewer sick days result in stable staffing and reduced emergency overtime. People with a high sense of belonging take 75 percent fewer sick days.[35]

Stable attendance protects customer service and eliminates the need for expensive temporary staffing. The Surgeon General's workplace mental health framework identifies connection and community as essentials, supporting what the operational data already shows.[36]

---

33 S. Ellis and J. Yarker, "Speak-Up Cultures: Creating Psychological Safety," *Harvard Business Review* (2019).

34 A. C. Edmondson and Z. Lei, "Psychological Safety: The History, Renaissance, and Future of an Interpersonal Construct," *Annual Review of Organizational Psychology and Organizational Behavior* 1, no. 1 (2014): 23–43, https://doi.org/10.1146/annurev-orgpsych-031413-091305.

35 BetterUp, 2024.

36 Office of the U.S. Surgeon General, *Framework for Workplace Mental Health and Well-Being* (U.S. Department of Health & Human Services, 2022).

Chapter 2: Why I Keep Having the Same Conversation with CFOs

Catching Problems Early

Most operational disasters begin as minor issues that often go unnoticed—safety shortcuts, compliance gaps, and minor client concerns that escalate into significant churn. Psychological safety creates early warning systems for these risks. When people feel safe speaking up, they catch and fix problems before they explode.[37]

Speak-up cultures require specific leader behaviors that sustain these conditions.[38] The result: fewer surprises, faster problem resolution, and lower risk of lawsuits, regulatory penalties, or reputation damage.

How the Measurement System Works

The measurement system makes this practical rather than theoretical. The Belonging Standard defines what to measure. The audit shows where you are and identifies the biggest gaps. The maturity model sequences improvements so you don't try to do everything at once. The platform tracks progress continuously and feeds insights back into the system.

This closed loop keeps effort focused on what matters most. Leaders track both backward-looking metrics, such as turnover and incident rates, and forward-looking metrics, including pillar scores and voice frequency. Together, they enable prevention and quick correction.

CFOs can translate improvements in belonging into dollars saved through three channels: avoided replacement costs, reduced downtime from absences and rework, and recovered

---

[37] Edmondson, 1999.
[38] Ellis & Yarker, 2019.

opportunities from faster cycle times.³⁹ BetterUp estimates $52 million in annual productivity and retention value for a ten-thousand-employee organization—a benchmark you can adjust using your own cost structure.⁴⁰

Governance That Sustains the Gains

Belonging improvements stick when you track them in the same meetings where you review revenue and margins. Include belonging scores by pillar and department in quarterly business reviews to keep leadership focused on what drives the results. The Surgeon General's workplace mental health framework provides policy support for investing in connection, meaning, and safety.⁴¹

This policy clarity enables legal, HR, and operations to work toward the same goals, rather than running competing initiatives. When belonging metrics appear alongside financial data in executive reviews, it signals that culture is everyone's responsibility, not just HR's.⁴²

These improvements reinforce each other. Fewer people quit, so senior people spend less time training replacements and more time innovating. Better attendance stabilizes project timelines, improving overall productivity. When people speak up early, you catch problems before they require expensive fixes. Each improvement makes the others stronger.⁴³

---

39 BetterUp, 2024.
40 BetterUp, 2024.
41 Office of the U.S. Surgeon General, 2022.
42 Deloitte, 2025.
43 BetterUp, 2024.

This is how belonging works: It helps teams perform better while reducing operational risks.[44]

You Can't Ignore This Anymore

Belonging is a necessary infrastructure, not optional cultural work. Organizations with strong belonging outperform during crises. They adapt more quickly, execute more effectively during change, and maintain performance when markets crash.[45]

As long as you employ humans, you need conditions that let people perform at their best. Without belonging infrastructure, people can't reach their potential.[46]

The evidence is consistent across every level: Belonging stabilizes performance and reduces organizational friction. CFOs can model retention savings with precision. CEOs can track belonging metrics alongside revenue. Employees respond to systems that reduce risk, enable learning, and reinforce purpose.[47] Belonging simultaneously improves retention, productivity, health, and risk management.[48]

The reality is simple: Belonging is a necessary infrastructure, not optional culture programming. Belonging drives retention, accelerates execution, enhances health outcomes, and mitigates operational risk.

CFOs invest in belonging when you show them dollars saved, not cultural programs. However, to understand why

---

44 Bain & Company, *Resilience as a Competitive Advantage* (2022), https://www.bain.com/insights.
45 Deloitte, 2025.
46 BetterUp, 2019.
47 Edmondson, 1999.
48 Catalyst, 2025.

those dollars are saved—and to build belonging systems that actually work—you need to understand the biological reality that explains everything I've been observing.

CHAPTER 3

What the Science Actually Tells Us

I didn't start my career with a focus on neuroscience or evolutionary psychology. I wanted to understand why some teams thrived while others struggled, and why certain managers could inspire their teams to perform at their best, while others saw talent leave.

After years of seeing the same patterns repeat, I began to delve into the research. Biological research explained the workplace patterns I'd been seeing.

Why Exclusion Literally Hurts

When I began researching exclusion, I discovered something startling: Brain imaging studies indicate that social exclusion activates the same neural regions that process physical pain.[49]

---

[49] N. I. Eisenberger, M. D. Lieberman, and K. D. Williams, "Does Rejection Hurt? An fMRI Study of Social Exclusion," *Science* 302, no. 5643 (2003): 290–292, https://doi.org/10.1126/science.1089134.

The 56% Solution

The brain literally treats rejection as a form of injury. Follow-up studies confirmed these mechanisms operate across all social contexts, explaining why workplace exclusion feels destabilizing even when there's no economic threat.[50]

This explained something I'd been seeing for years: why talented people would suddenly become defensive or withdrawn after seemingly minor interactions. A dismissive comment in a meeting, an overlooked idea, or being left off an email thread triggered the brain's threat detection system.[51]

When that happens, the prefrontal cortex, the part of the brain responsible for complex thinking, creativity, and collaboration, is hijacked. Blood flow shifts to more primitive survival circuits. Decision-making becomes impaired, and learning shuts down. John Cacioppo and Louise Hawkley[52] documented how perceived social isolation disrupts cognitive functioning, creating a hypervigilant state that narrows attention and impairs decision-making. The skills you hired them for become inaccessible when their brains prioritize survival. The skills you hired them for get suppressed by their brain's threat response.[53]

Once again, the pattern is evident. The engineer stopped contributing ideas after her suggestions were repeatedly ignored. The manager became micromanaging and rigid after a public

---

50 M. D. Lieberman and N. I. Eisenberger, "Pains and Pleasures of Social Life," *Science* 323, no. 5916 (2009): 890–891, https://doi.org/10.1126/science.1170008.

51 Eisenberger et al., 2003.

52 J. T. Cacioppo and L. C. Hawkley, "Perceived Social Isolation and Cognition," *Trends in Cognitive Sciences* 13, no. 10 (2009): 447–454, https://doi.org/10.1016/j.tics.2009.05.005.

53 N. I. Eisenberger, "The Pain of Social Disconnection: Examining the Shared Neural Underpinnings of Physical and Social Pain," *Nature Reviews Neuroscience* 13 (2012): 421–434, https://doi.org/10.1038/nrn3231.

criticism. The entire team went silent after a poorly handled reorganization.

Their brains were doing exactly what evolution shaped them to do: focus on survival rather than performance.[54]

Healthcare research provides the clearest evidence for belonging's operational impact. Studies across hospital systems have shown that teams with higher psychological safety report medical errors 47 percent more frequently than control groups, with error reporting directly correlating with patient safety outcomes and reduced malpractice exposure.[55] The mechanism operates through threat detection suppression: When staff trust that reporting problems won't trigger retaliation, organizations catch failures before they compound into crises.

Edmondson's foundational research establishes psychological safety as the strongest predictor of team learning velocity, with effects measurable within thirty to sixty days of intervention (Edmondson, 1999, 2019). Teams scoring in the top quartile for psychological safety generate 67 percent more improvement suggestions and implement process changes 40 percent faster than teams in the bottom quartile. The cognitive mechanisms are consistent across industries—when threat detection isn't consuming mental resources, people contribute more readily to problem-solving and innovation.

---

54 Eisenberger, 2012.

55 A. Newman, R. Donohue, and N. Eva, "Psychological Safety: A Systematic Review of the Literature," *Human Resource Management Review* 27, no. 3 (2017): 521–535; AHRQ, *Annual Perspective: Psychological Safety for Healthcare Staff* (Agency for Healthcare Research and Quality, 2023), https://psnet.ahrq.gov/perspective/annual-perspective-psychological-safety-healthcare-staff.

How Trust Rewires the System

When people experience consistent signals of safety and inclusion, neurochemical pathways are activated. Roger Mayer, James Davis, and F. David Schoorman[56] demonstrated that trust comprises three essential elements: ability, benevolence, and integrity. Without all three, people default to self-protection mode regardless of policies or training.

When organizations break trust, they can't talk their way back. Peter Eberl, Daniel Geiger, and Michael Aßländer[57] tracked companies after major integrity failures and found that words don't rebuild trust, actions do, and only when they're consistent over months.

Oxytocin levels rise, which enhances cooperation and reduces stress responses.[58] Dopamine pathways strengthen, improving learning and motivation.[59]

Transformation is evident when working with teams that get belonging right. People sit differently in meetings, more relaxed and engaged. They interrupt each other constructively instead of waiting for permission to speak. Ideas build on each other instead of competing.

Paul Zak's research on the neurochemistry of trust gave me the framework to understand what I was observing. In high-trust environments, people's brains produce more oxytocin, which

---

56 R. C. Mayer, J. H. Davis, and F. D. Schoorman, "An Integrative Model of Organizational Trust," *Academy of Management Review* 20, no. 3 (1995): 709–734, https://doi.org/10.5465/amr.1995.9508080335.

57 P. Eberl, D. Geiger, and M. S. Aßländer, "Repairing Trust in an Organization after Integrity Violations: The Ambivalence of Organizational Rule Adjustments," *Organization Studies* 36, no. 9 (2015): 1205–1235, https://doi.org/10.1177/0170840615585335.

58 P. J. Zak, "The Neuroscience of Trust," *Harvard Business Review* (2017).

59 Lieberman & Eisenberger, 2009.

is correlated with greater generosity, improved collaboration, and an increased willingness to take interpersonal risks.[60] Zak's research measured actual oxytocin levels in high-trust teams, providing biological evidence for the impact of trust.

When people feel genuinely supported at work, their stress response actually changes. Studies reveal oxytocin doesn't just make us more cooperative, it helps buffer the physical impact of stress when we know our colleagues have our backs.

You can see this play out in real teams. Groups with strong relationships tend to perform well under pressure, while those who feel isolated often fall apart quickly. There's even measurable evidence: Cortisol levels drop significantly when people receive support from trusted coworkers versus facing problems alone.

That's why investing in genuine connection becomes more important during tough times, not less. People literally function better when they're not dealing with stress alone.

The Social Identity Connection

The psychology research filled in another piece of the puzzle. Henri Tajfel and John Turner's work on social identity theory demonstrated that people derive their sense of self, in part, from group membership. When a membership feels secure and valued, individuals invest more energy in the group's success. When it feels threatened or marginal, they redirect energy toward self-protection.[61]

---

60 Zak, 2017.
61 H. Tajfel and J. C. Turner, "An Integrative Theory of Intergroup Conflict," in *The Social Psychology of Intergroup Relations*, ed. W. G. Austin and S. Worchel (Brooks/Cole, 1979), 33–47.

I'd seen this play out countless times in reorganizations and mergers. Teams that felt their identity was respected during change adapted quickly and maintained performance. But marginalized teams became defensive, hoarded information, and lost productivity for months.

Leon Festinger's studies showed that cohesive groups have higher commitment, lower absenteeism, and more consistent standards. But cohesion requires structural conditions that reinforce shared identity and mutual dependence.[62]

This explains why some diversity initiatives fail while others succeed. Adding different people to a team doesn't automatically create inclusion. Without systems that provide psychological safety, enabling people to speak up and seek support, diversity can actually increase tension.[63]

The Evolutionary Foundation

The evolutionary research explained why belonging hits so hard and so fast. From an evolutionary perspective, group membership was a survival issue. Humans who couldn't maintain group inclusion faced dramatically lower survival odds.[64] Maslow[65] positioned belonging immediately above physiological and safety needs in his hierarchy, arguing that without social connection, people cannot progress toward higher-order functioning.

Humans became incredibly good at reading social cues because our survival depended on it. We're constantly scanning

---

62 L. Festinger, "Informal Social Communication," *Psychological Review* 57, no. 5 (1950): 271–282, https://doi.org/10.1037/h0056932.
63 Edmondson & Lei, 2014.
64 Baumeister & Leary, 1995.
65 Maslow, 1943.

Chapter 3: What the Science Actually Tells Us

for cues about our status, safety, and acceptance in any group. These assessments happen below conscious awareness and influence everything from stress hormones to cognitive capacity.

Robert Trivers's work on reciprocal altruism showed how cooperation evolved as a survival strategy. Groups with stronger internal collaboration could coordinate resources more effectively, defend against threats, and adapt to environmental changes. The groups that figured out belonging outcompeted the ones that didn't.[66]

In modern organizations, this translates directly. Departments with high belonging coordinate better during crises, share information more freely, and recover faster from setbacks. The evolutionary logic still applies—cooperation separates winners from losers.

The SCARF Model in Practice

David Rock's SCARF model explains why certain management practices consistently evoke defensiveness in people. SCARF[67] identifies five social domains: Status, Certainty, Autonomy, Relatedness, and Fairness.

Reorganizations that demoted people without a clear rationale triggered status threats. Strategic changes announced without timelines created specific threats. Micromanagement during high-pressure periods destroyed autonomy.

Each threat triggered predictable responses: withdrawal,

---

[66] R. L. Trivers, "The Evolution of Reciprocal Altruism," *Quarterly Review of Biology* 46, no. 1 (1971): 35–57, https://doi.org/10.1086/406755.

[67] D. Rock, "SCARF: A Brain-Based Model for Collaborating with and Influencing Others," *NeuroLeadership Journal* 1 (2008): 44–52.

defensive behavior, reduced collaboration, and eventual disengagement or departure.[68]

Relatedness maps directly to belonging; when employees experience exclusion or disconnection, the brain's threat circuitry (including the amygdala) becomes active, impairing prefrontal cortex functions such as problem-solving and impulse control.[69]

The same framework explains positive triggers. Practices that enhance status, certainty, autonomy, relatedness, and fairness activate reward circuits. Performance improves, learning accelerates, and discretionary effort increases.[70]

Why This Matters for System Design

Understanding the biological and psychological foundations of belonging changed how I approach organizational design. Instead of hoping people would get along better, I designed processes that worked with how neuroscience actually functions.[71] Predictable communication patterns reduce certainty threats. Structured decision-making processes address fairness concerns. Clear role definitions and growth pathways protect status and autonomy. Cross-functional collaboration rituals strengthen relatedness.

When these elements are integrated into how work is performed, belonging becomes built into the way work is done, as opposed to being dependent on individual personalities. It doesn't depend on having naturally collaborative personalities

---

68 Rock, 2008.
69 Lieberman & Eisenberger, 2009.
70 Rock, 2008.
71 Rock, 2008.

or charismatic leaders. It depends on creating conditions that allow human beings to function at their neurological and psychological best.[72]

The Convergence

What strikes me most about reviewing this research is how all three levels—neuroscience, psychology, and evolutionary biology—point to the same conclusion. Human beings are wired for connection, cooperation, and contribution.[73] When organizational systems align with how people naturally work, teams share problems more quickly and adapt more effectively. When they work against these patterns, performance degrades just as predictably.[74]

Belonging is a concept that must be measured like any other organizational capability. It's about creating structural conditions that work with human biology rather than against it. The five pillars of the Belonging Standard—Psychological Safety, Inclusion, Support, Connection, and Purpose—directly address the neurological, psychological, and evolutionary patterns I've described.[75]

Trust is a critical output of this system: When leaders invest in fair, supportive, and transparent practices, organizational trust grows, which further amplifies cooperation and group adaptability.[76]

---

72 Eisenberger, 2012.
73 Baumeister & Leary, 1995.
74 Lieberman & Eisenberger, 2009.
75 Edmondson & Lei, 2014.
76 Mayer, Davis, & Schoorman, 1995.

Scientific Validation Across Disciplines

The research across neuroscience, psychology, and evolutionary biology converges on a single principle: Human performance optimizes when organizational systems align with fundamental social and cognitive patterns. This convergence provides the scientific foundation for systematizing belonging as measurable infrastructure rather than treating it as abstract culture work.

The Science Behind Why Belonging Works

Three streams of research—psychology, neuroscience, and evolutionary biology—all point to the same conclusion: Social connection drives performance in measurable ways.

Psychology research shows that people cooperate and share information more readily when they feel part of a group. Tajfel and Turner's social identity theory demonstrates that group membership drives cooperation, while Festinger's work on group cohesion links belonging to higher commitment and goal achievement.[77] In practice, this means employees with trusted colleagues show higher productivity, faster knowledge transfer, and stronger team resilience.

Neuroscience supports this at the biological level. Positive social interactions trigger the release of oxytocin, which enhances cooperation and reduces stress.[78] Social connection literally activates reward pathways in the brain, which improves collaboration. When people feel safe, their brains can focus cognitive resources on problem-solving instead of threat detection. Teams with psychological safety surface problems earlier, iterate faster, and maintain performance under pressure.

---

77 Tajfel & Turner, 1979; Festinger, 1950.
78 Zak, 2017.

Chapter 3: What the Science Actually Tells Us

Evolutionary biology explains why these patterns exist. Reciprocal altruism and group selection show that cooperative groups consistently outcompete individualistic ones. Our brains evolved to optimize performance when we feel secure in a group membership. Organizations with strong trust infrastructure demonstrate faster adaptation to market changes, higher innovation rates, and more resilient recovery from setbacks.

Research Integration Insight: Across all disciplines, belonging emerges as an infrastructure that optimizes human performance by working in harmony with biological and psychological design, rather than against it. The five-pillar framework translates this converging evidence into measurable organizational systems.

The framework operationalizes these insights by embedding measurement and intervention into the five pillars of the Belonging Standard, translating psychological, neurological, and evolutionary evidence into specific behaviors for leaders and managers.

The neuroscience research explains why belonging matters biologically, but knowing why doesn't solve the practical problem I kept encountering: Most organizations can't even define what belonging means, let alone measure it.

What the Science Actually Tells Us

The neuroscience research explains patterns I'd been seeing for years: Social exclusion activates the same brain regions as physical pain, literally hijacking the cognitive resources people need for complex thinking and collaboration. When people lack trust in their environment, their mental energy is diverted from problem-solving to threat detection. But neuroscience research doesn't solve the practical problem I kept encountering.

Trust requires three elements—competence, care, and consistency—and missing any one of these puts people in a state of self-protection, regardless of policies or training. It is biology that explains why belonging systems either work with human brain function or waste money fighting against it.

Most leaders can't define belonging consistently across their teams, let alone measure it. Ask five executives what belonging means and you get five different answers. Ask them how to measure it and you get blank stares. You can't manage what you can't measure, and you can't measure what you can't define with precision.

CHAPTER 4

The Framework That Actually Works

The neuroscience research explains why belonging matters biologically, but knowing why doesn't solve the practical problem I kept observing: Most organizations can't even define what belonging means. Ask five leaders what belonging means, and you'll get five different answers. Ask them how to measure it, and you'll get blank stares.[79]

You can't manage what you can't measure, and you can't measure what you can't define clearly.[80]

That's why I developed the Belonging Standard, not as an academic exercise, but as a practical necessity. This approach builds on established principles from organizational development research,[81] but translates them into something leaders can

---

79 Deloitte, 2025.
80 Deloitte, 2025.
81 R. F. DeVellis, *Scale Development: Theory and Applications*, 4th ed. (Sage, 2017).

actually use. I needed a framework that was precise enough to measure, specific enough to act on, and comprehensive enough to create real change.[82]

Why Most Belonging Efforts Fail

The three problems that repeatedly kill belonging initiatives:

1 **Inconsistent definitions:** Different departments, different leaders, different interpretations. Marketing talks about "authentic selves," HR focuses on "psychological safety," Operations wants "team cohesion." Everyone's working toward different goals.[83]

2 **Lack of measurability:** Without specific indicators, belonging remains a feeling rather than a condition. You can't correlate feelings with retention, performance, or innovation. You can't build a business case on sentiment.[84]

3 **No implementation road map:** Leaders acknowledge the importance of belonging, but they are unsure about where to begin, what to prioritize, or how to time the interventions.[85]

The Belonging Standard solves all three problems by breaking belonging into five measurable, manageable components that work together as a system.[86]

---

82 Edmondson & Lei, 2014.
83 Deloitte, 2025.
84 BetterUp, 2019.
85 BetterUp, 2024.
86 Edmondson & Lei, 2014.

Chapter 4: The Framework That Actually Works

Three completely different fields of study—psychology, neuroscience, and evolutionary biology—all point to the same conclusion about human performance in groups.

Henri Tajfel and John Turner's work on social identity theory reveals that people derive their sense of self partly from group membership.[87] When that membership feels secure, they invest energy in the group's success. When it feels threatened, they redirect that energy toward self-protection. This exact pattern plays out in every reorganization.

The neuroscience research fills in the missing pieces. Brain imaging studies reveal that social exclusion activates the same neural regions that process physical pain.[88] When Alicia's suggestions got ignored repeatedly, her brain was literally treating that exclusion as injury. Her defensive and withdrawn behavior wasn't a character flaw—her prefrontal cortex was being hijacked by threat detection circuits.[89]

The research validates what happens in organizations every day. The five pillars aren't arbitrary—they map directly onto fundamental human needs that have been validated across multiple disciplines.

The Five Pillars That Matter

Throughout my career, working across various sectors, I've observed that belonging consistently manifests in five specific ways. When these conditions are consistently present, people perform at their best. When they're missing or inconsistent,

---

[87] Tajfel & Turner, 1979.
[88] Eisenberger, Lieberman, & Williams, 2003.
[89] Eisenberger, 2012.

even high performers start protecting themselves instead of pushing boundaries.[90]

1 Psychological Safety

Definition and Behaviors

Psychological Safety is the foundation condition where people can speak up, share concerns, admit mistakes, and challenge ideas without fear of interpersonal risk or career penalty. It's the confidence that you won't be punished or humiliated for speaking up with ideas, questions, concerns, or mistakes.

When I was leading talent at an Ohio Fortune 500 company, the CEO told me, "You know, I know that I'm not being told the truth. I know that it's not by design; however, people filter for what they think I want to hear as opposed to what I need to hear." The irony is that I didn't feel I had the psychological safety to tell him that his leadership team might not have psychological safety either.

Psychological safety requires more than permission—it demands structural protection. Kahn[91] identified psychological safety as one of three core conditions for engagement, alongside meaningfulness and availability—establishing that people evaluate interpersonal risk before choosing to engage fully at work.

Observable behaviors include the following:

- People openly share concerns and mistakes in team meetings.

---

90 Edmondson, 1999.

91 W. A. Kahn, "Psychological Conditions of Personal Engagement and Disengagement at Work," *Academy of Management Journal* 33, no. 4 (1990): 692–724, https://doi.org/10.2307/256287.

- Leaders admit their own fallibility and actively invite input from all levels.
- Disagreements get raised and addressed constructively rather than avoided.
- Team members ask questions without fear of appearing incompetent.
- Feedback flows in all directions, focused on improvement rather than blame.

Neuroscience Validation

Naomi Eisenberger's research demonstrates why this pillar must come first: Social rejection activates the anterior cingulate cortex—the same region processing physical pain.[92] When people feel unsafe to speak up, their prefrontal cortex gets hijacked for threat detection instead of problem-solving.

You can't include someone whose brain is focused on survival rather than contribution. You can't provide meaningful support to someone who's afraid to admit they need help. You can't build genuine connections when people are in defensive mode.

Clark's research reveals that psychological safety develops through four sequential stages:

1 Inclusion safety (feeling included) →
2 Learner safety (safe to learn) →
3 Contributor safety (safe to contribute) →
4 Challenger safety (safe to challenge status quo).[93]

---

[92] Eisenberger, Lieberman, & Williams, 2003.
[93] T. R. Clark, *The Four Stages of Psychological Safety: Defining the Path to Inclusion and Innovation* (Berrett-Koehler, 2020).

Each stage requires the neurological foundation of the previous stage. Organizations often assume they can jump directly to challenger safety—encouraging people to speak truth to power—without first building the earlier stages.

Business Application

Edmondson's research shows how this plays out in teams.[94] The highest-performing groups weren't the ones with the smartest people or best resources. They were the ones where people could say "I don't know," "I made an error," or "I think we're missing something" without incurring a political penalty. Without that foundation, other belonging conditions become fragile.

Organizations with strong psychological safety see measurable improvements in the following:

- **Error detection and reporting:** Problems surface early instead of becoming crises.
- **Innovation rates:** People share ideas without filtering for political correctness.
- **Learning velocity:** Teams iterate faster because failures become learning opportunities.
- **Risk management:** Early escalation prevents small issues from becoming expensive disasters.

When psychological safety is missing, problems stay hidden until they become crises, learning stops, and the organization operates on incomplete information. Organizations that skip the foundational stages often find that their "open door policies" remain unused because people don't feel fundamentally safe to be vulnerable.

---

94 Edmondson, 1999.

Chapter 4: The Framework That Actually Works

The Alicia Test for Safety

Can new people surface concerns about processes or decisions without career penalty? If your newest team members aren't speaking up about problems they see, you have a safety issue, not a talent issue. Every organization has people like Alicia—technically competent but ignored when they try to contribute improvements.

2 Inclusion

Definition and Behaviors

Inclusion means diverse perspectives actively influence decisions and outcomes, not just get invited to the conversation. It's the degree to which different viewpoints, backgrounds, and approaches shape how work gets done and decisions get made.

Most "inclusive" processes collect input from everyone, then make decisions the same way they always have. Mallick's research identifies this as one of the most common inclusion myths: confusing diverse representation in meetings with actual influence over outcomes.[95] Real inclusion means input actually influences decisions, not just gets collected.

Inclusion requires that the people making decisions represent the people affected by those decisions. Butler, Kleinbaum, et al. demonstrate that inclusion requires not only formal diversity but also ensuring that diverse individuals have genuine influence on decisions.[96] Differing views get documented, considered, and addressed, rather than being politely noted and ignored.

---

[95] M. Mallick, *Reimagine Inclusion: Debunking 13 Myths to Transform Your Workplace* (Wiley, 2023).

[96] T. Butler, E. Falk, and A. M. Kleinbaum, *Belonging in Organizational Networks: Integrating Psychological and Social Network Perspectives on Inclusion* (Working Paper, University of Pennsylvania & Dartmouth College, 2024), https://faculty.tuck.dartmouth.edu/images/uploads/faculty/adam-kleinbaum/Workplace_Inclusion.pdf.

Observable behaviors include the following:

- Diverse perspectives are actively sought and integrated into decision-making processes.
- Recognition is distributed equitably across different groups and working styles.
- Meeting structures ensure every voice gets heard before decisions are finalized.
- Ideas from underrepresented groups get documented, evaluated, and implemented at similar rates.
- Policies and practices address the needs of diverse workforce segments.

Neuroscience Validation

David Rock's SCARF research reveals that "Status" and "Fairness" are fundamental social needs.[97] When people's perspectives are genuinely valued (not just heard), it activates reward pathways that enhance motivation and learning. Tokenism—bringing diverse people into meetings without letting them influence decisions—creates a Status threat that impairs their cognitive performance.

The brain's reward system responds to genuine impact, not symbolic participation. When people see their input shape outcomes, it activates the same neural pathways that drive engagement and discretionary effort.

Different brains process information differently, creating richer analysis and more robust solutions when multiple perspectives are genuinely integrated rather than just consulted.

---

97 Rock, 2008.

Chapter 4: The Framework That Actually Works

Business Application

McKinsey research links inclusive cultures directly to business results: higher innovation revenue and above-average profitability.[98] Multiple viewpoints broaden perspective and catch assumptions that homogeneous teams miss.

Organizations with strong inclusion see the following:

- **Higher decision quality:** Diverse perspectives reveal overlooked areas and groupthink.
- **Increased innovation throughput:** Different approaches generate more creative solutions.
- **Reduced bias-related risk:** Multiple viewpoints catch assumptions homogeneous teams miss.
- **Better market responsiveness:** Diverse teams understand diverse customer needs more effectively.

The Alicia Test for Inclusion

Do workflow improvement suggestions from capable people actually get implemented? If good ideas from people like Alicia consistently get polite nods but no action, your inclusion infrastructure isn't working—you're collecting input without providing influence.

---

98 S. Dixon-Fyle, K. Dolan, V. Hunt, and S. Prince, *Diversity Wins: How Inclusion Matters* (McKinsey & Company, 2020), https://www.mckinsey.com/featured-insights/diversity-and-inclusion/diversity-wins-how-inclusion-matters.

3   Support

Definition and Behaviors

Support means resources, tools, guidance, and advocacy are available proactively, before people break down or burn out. It's about removing barriers and providing what people need to succeed.

In most organizations, support is something you have to request, justify, and wait for. By then, it's often too late. David R. May, Richard L. Gilson, and Lynne M. Harter[99] demonstrate that having the right resources available reduces stress and improves performance. The key is making support proactive, not reactive.

Strong support means managers proactively check workload and remove barriers rather than waiting for distress signals. Training, mentoring, and tools—including technical systems—are accessible without bureaucratic friction. Leaders advocate upward for their team's needs and resource requirements.

Observable behaviors include the following:

- Managers proactively check on workload and help remove obstacles.
- Training, development, and learning resources are accessible without bureaucratic friction.
- People receive timely help when they request guidance or assistance.
- Tool access, information, and resource allocation happen efficiently.

---

[99] D. R. May, R. L. Gilson, and L. M. Harter, "The Psychological Conditions of Meaningfulness, Safety, and Availability and the Engagement of the Human Spirit at Work," *Journal of Occupational and Organizational Psychology* 77, no. 1 (2004): 11–37, https://doi.org/10.1348/096317904322915892.

Chapter 4: The Framework That Actually Works

- Leaders advocate upward for their team's needs and resource requirements.

Neuroscience Validation

The Job Demands-Resources model has neurological foundations.[100] When job demands exceed available resources, the brain produces cortisol—the stress hormone that impairs memory, learning, and collaboration over time. Bakker and Demerouti's research shows this isn't just about workload; it's about whether people trust that help will be available when needed.

The Support pillar addresses this by making resource access predictable, which reduces cognitive load spent on "resource anxiety" and frees mental energy for productive work. When people know support is reliably available, their brains can focus on contribution rather than conservation.

Proactive support works better than reactive support because uncertainty about resource availability keeps the brain in scanning mode, constantly evaluating whether current demands are sustainable. Predictable support systems allow cognitive resources to focus on problem-solving rather than resource monitoring.

Business Application

Organizations with strong support systems achieve the following:

- **Reduced burnout and absenteeism:** People can sustain performance without breaking down.
- **Higher productivity during pressure periods:** Resources buffer against demand spikes.

---

100 E. Demerouti, A. B. Bakker, F. Nachreiner, and W. B. Schaufeli, "The Job Demands–Resources Model of Burnout," *Journal of Applied Psychology* 86, no. 3 (2001): 499–512, https://doi.org/10.1037/0021-9010.86.3.499.

- **Faster skill development:** Learning happens more efficiently when support is accessible.
- **Better retention of high performers:** People stay when they feel supported, not just compensated.

The Alicia Test for Support

Are resources and guidance available before people hit walls? Alicia had the technical skills but lacked context about team dynamics and unwritten rules. If people like Alicia are struggling silently rather than getting proactive help, your support infrastructure needs strengthening.

4 Connection

Definition and Behaviors

Connection refers to trust-based relationships that extend beyond immediate job requirements. It's the presence of genuine professional relationships built on mutual respect, shared purpose, and collaborative problem-solving.

Workplace relationships built on mutual respect and genuine care create different organizational outcomes than routine task-focused interactions.[101] Even brief but meaningful workplace interactions create measurable benefits for individuals and teams. Quality matters more than quantity—it's the difference between transactional cooperation and genuine collaboration.

Connections don't happen accidentally in busy environments. They require intentional design.

---

[101] J. E. Dutton and E. D. Heaphy, "The Power of High-Quality Connections," in *Positive Organizational Scholarship*, ed. K. S. Cameron, J. E. Dutton, and R. E. Quinn (Berrett-Koehler, 2003), 263–278.

Observable behaviors include the following:

- People have trusted colleagues they turn to for advice, guidance, and collaboration.
- Cross-functional relationships form naturally and get reinforced through work processes.
- Leaders invest time in relationship building that goes beyond task management.
- Information and knowledge sharing happen freely across organizational boundaries.
- Teams collaborate on projects and challenges without requiring management coordination.

Neuroscience Validation

Paul Zak's research on the "trust molecule" reveals why Connection can't be left to chance.[102] Oxytocin—released during positive social interactions—doesn't just make people feel good; it measurably improves their ability to do the following:

- Share information openly without hoarding for competitive advantage.
- Give others the benefit of the doubt during conflicts and misunderstandings.
- Take calculated risks for team benefit rather than individual protection.

The brain chemistry of collaboration needs intentional cultivation. Social disconnection activates the same neural

---

102 Zak, 2017.

networks as physical injury, literally hurting cognitive function and collaboration capacity.[103] This explains why teams without genuine relationships break down under pressure—the brain processes isolation as a threat.

Connection multiplies other pillar effects: When people trust each other, they're more willing to be vulnerable (Safety), more likely to share diverse perspectives (Inclusion), more comfortable asking for help (Support), and more motivated by shared goals (Purpose).

Business Application

Organizations with strong connection demonstrate the following:

- **Higher cross-functional collaboration effectiveness:** Projects succeed because relationships enable coordination.
- **Faster knowledge transfer and institutional learning:** Information flows through trusted networks.
- **Lower coordination costs:** Relationships reduce the management overhead needed for teamwork.
- **Enhanced organizational resilience:** Connected teams support each other through challenges.

Without connection, coordination costs increase, knowledge transfer slows, and teams become brittle under pressure. With it, collaboration becomes easier, faster, and more resilient because people can focus cognitive resources on problem-solving rather than on threat detection.

---

103 Eisenberger, 2012.

The Alicia Test for Connection

Do new people develop working relationships beyond task-level interactions? Alicia completed her assignments but never formed the informal networks that would have helped her navigate team politics and amplify her ideas. If capable people like Alicia remain professionally isolated despite doing good work, your connection infrastructure is missing the relationship-building mechanisms that make collaboration natural.

5 Purpose

Definition and Behaviors

Purpose is about understanding how individual work contributes to meaningful outcomes and having that contribution be recognized and valued. It's a clear line of sight between daily tasks and impact that matters, combined with recognition that reinforces that connection.

Meaning at work comes from understanding how your contribution fits the bigger picture, not from motivational posters.[104] Meaningful work has become a key driver of economic value, not just employee satisfaction.[105] Organizations with clear purpose alignment experience measurable productivity advantages over those relying solely on traditional motivation.[106]

Purpose emerges when employees can articulate how their work aligns with organizational goals, when recognition links

---

[104] Rosso, B. D., Dekas, K. H., & Wrzesniewski, A. (2010). On the meaning of work: A theoretical integration and review. *Research in Organizational Behavior*, *30*, 91–127. https://doi.org/10.1016/j.riob.2010.09.001.

[105] A. Hurst, *The Purpose Economy* (Elevate, 2014).

[106] Institute for Corporate Productivity (i4cp), *The Productivity Predicament: Executive Brief* (2024), https://go.i4cp.com/hubfs/Download%20Assets/2024%20Priorities%20and%20Predictions%20Report%20-%20i4cp.pdf.

individual achievements to the mission's impact, and when decision-making communicates the value of different roles throughout the organization.

Observable behaviors include the following:

- People can articulate how their work contributes to organizational goals and customer outcomes.
- Recognition explicitly connects individual achievements to mission impact.
- Decision-making communication helps people understand the value of their specific roles.
- Leaders regularly reinforce the meaning and importance of different types of work.
- Performance discussions focus on impact and contribution, not just task completion.

Neuroscience Validation

Viktor Frankl's observations about meaning and motivation now have neurological validation. When people understand how their work contributes to something larger, it activates the brain's reward system and creates what researchers call "eudaimonic well-being"—the satisfaction that comes from meaningful contribution.

Michael Pratt and Blake Ashforth's research shows this isn't about inspirational speeches; it's about clear cognitive connections between daily tasks and valued outcomes.[107] The Purpose pillar provides the specific mechanisms that help brains make

---

107 M. G. Pratt and B. E. Ashforth, "Fostering Meaningfulness in Working and at Work," in *Positive Organizational Scholarship*, ed. K. S. Cameron, J. E. Dutton, and R. E. Quinn (Berrett-Koehler, 2003), 309–327.

Chapter 4: The Framework That Actually Works

these connections. The neurological reward system responds to perceived impact, not just stated purpose.

Purpose must be both personal and reinforced: The brain needs to understand the connection (cognitive component) and receive validation that the contribution matters (emotional component). Purpose without recognition feels empty; recognition without purpose feels shallow.

Business Application

When purpose is clear and reinforced, people give extra effort, quit less often, and adapt more readily to change because they understand why it matters.

Organizations with strong purpose alignment see the following:

- **Higher discretionary effort:** People go beyond minimum requirements when they see impact.
- **Lower voluntary turnover:** Meaningful work creates stronger commitment than compensation alone.
- **Better adaptability during change:** Shared purpose helps people navigate uncertainty and ambiguity.
- **Increased resilience during difficult periods:** Understanding "why" sustains motivation when "how" gets challenging.

The Alicia Test for Purpose

Can people see how their contributions matter to the bigger picture? Alicia understood her job requirements but couldn't see why her workflow improvements would benefit anyone or connect to team goals. If people like Alicia are executing tasks without understanding their impact or receiving recognition for their value, your purpose infrastructure needs development.

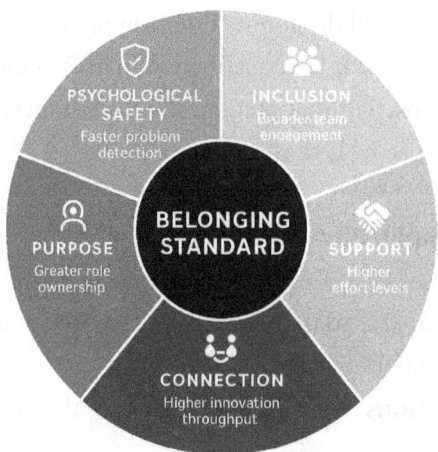

Cultural Context and Framework Adaptation

While the five pillars represent universal human needs, their expression and implementation must be adapted to cultural context. Recent SAGE journal research demonstrates that **universal applicability of belonging frameworks is limited**—success is context dependent across national, industry, and team-level cultures.

For example:

1 **Psychological Safety** may require different behavioral norms in high-context versus low-context cultures.
2 **Inclusion** practices that work in individualistic cultures may need adaptation for collectivistic environments.
3 **Support** systems and resources vary across cultures in terms of hierarchy, mentorship approaches, and

expectations for individual versus collective responsibility for development.

4 **Connection** building varies significantly across cultures with different relationship and hierarchy norms.

5 **Purpose** alignment requires understanding cultural values about individual achievement versus collective contribution.

This cultural sensitivity requirement requires thoughtful local adaptation of the framework. Organizations implementing belonging across multiple cultures need region-specific pillar indicators while maintaining consistent measurement methodology.

Industry-Specific Adaptation Requirements

The five pillars work across industries, but they look different in practice. Healthcare teams need psychological safety to report errors without getting fired. Tech companies need inclusion processes that actually use diverse technical perspectives, not just collect them. Schools need support systems that work with academic calendars and student development stages.

Healthcare

Patient safety depends on people speaking up about problems. Psychological Safety becomes about life-and-death reporting. Support systems must handle the stress of critical decisions. Connection matters because poor care coordination kills people.

Technology

Innovation requires failure, so Psychological Safety must allow rapid iteration without blame. Inclusion means diverse technical perspectives actually influence product decisions. Purpose alignment helps engineers see how their code affects real users.

Education
Support systems follow academic cycles rather than business quarters. Connection building serves learning goals, not just team cohesion. Different achievement patterns matter more than corporate metrics.

Manufacturing
Safety includes physical hazards alongside psychological ones. Connection must work across shifts and plant locations. Support addresses both operational problems and career development.

Each industry changes how the pillars work, but the same five conditions determine whether people contribute fully or protect themselves.

Cultural Context and Global Implementation

National and organizational cultures strongly affect how belonging is experienced and fostered. Research on optimal distinctiveness theory highlights how **both individual uniqueness and group belonging must be balanced**, but this balance is interpreted differently across cultures.

Cultural Adaptation Requirements

- **High-Context vs. Low-Context Cultures:** Psychological Safety may require different behavioral norms—direct feedback in low-context cultures versus indirect communication in high-context cultures. Inclusion practices

Chapter 4: The Framework That Actually Works

must account for cultural differences in voice, hierarchy, and decision-making participation.
- **Individualistic vs. Collectivistic Orientations:** Connection building varies significantly based on cultural relationship norms. Support systems may emphasize individual development in individualistic cultures versus group harmony in collectivistic cultures.
- **Power-Distance Variations:** Inclusion practices that work in low power-distance cultures (encouraging challenge to authority) may be counterproductive in high power-distance cultures without careful adaptation.
- **Global Implementation Strategy:** For organizations with diverse workforces or global teams, research-backed frameworks recommend investing in cultural learning and regular feedback to ensure belonging initiatives are relevant in each context. This requires the following:
  o Local adaptation of pillar indicators while maintaining measurement consistency.
  o Culture-specific manager training and competency development.
  o Regular feedback loops to ensure practices remain culturally appropriate.

The framework's strength lies in providing universal structure while enabling cultural customization in implementation.

Why Most Culture Measurement Fails

Most organizations rely on sentiment analysis when they need structural diagnosis.

Al-Twairesh and colleagues' research shows the limitations

of sentiment analysis—it captures feelings, not the conditions that create those feelings.[108] When you ask "How do you feel about belonging?" you're measuring outcomes, not the structural conditions that determine whether someone actually belongs.

That's backward. Feelings tell you what happened. Structure tells you what's going to happen next.

The structural approach builds on Kenneth Bollen's work on latent variables.[109] Belonging operates as something you can't measure directly, you have to infer it from what people actually do. When someone like Alicia stops contributing ideas after her suggestions get ignored, that's a structural indicator of inclusion problems, not just individual dissatisfaction.

Rex Kline's latest work on structural equation modeling shows how the five pillars influence each other as a system.[110] When Safety scores drop, it predictably affects Inclusion and Connection scores. Most employee surveys miss these relationships because they treat each question as separate.

How the Five Pillars Work Together: Systems Neuroscience

Individual neuroscience findings don't explain why all five pillars are necessary. The answer lies in systems neuroscience—how different brain networks interact to create emergent properties.

---

[108] N. Al-Twairesh, H. Al-Negheimish, and A. M. Al-Salman, "Surface and Deep Features Ensemble for Sentiment Analysis of Arabic Tweets," *IEEE Access* 11 (2023): 84122–84131, https://doi.org/10.1109/ACCESS.2023.3414097.

[109] K. A. Bollen, *Structural Equations with Latent Variables* (New York: Wiley, 1989).

[110] R. B. Kline, *Principles and Practice of Structural Equation Modeling*, 5th ed. (New York: Guilford Press, 2023).

Chapter 4: The Framework That Actually Works

The Threat Override Effect
If any pillar is weak, it can trigger threat responses that override the benefits of strong pillars. Neurobiological research on multisensory threat integration shows that when organizational safety breaks down, threat responses dominate even where strong support systems exist.

The amygdala can override the benefits of excellent Support, Connection, or Purpose when it perceives Safety or Inclusion threats. This explains why Psychological Safety is the first pillar. Without it, people's brains remain in protective mode regardless of other positive conditions.

The Amplification Effect
When multiple pillars are strong, they create neurochemical conditions that amplify each other. Barbara Fredrickson's "broaden-and-build" theory shows that positive emotions—created when conditions like safety, inclusion, and support coincide—expand cognitive capacity and build psychological resources over time.[111]

These upward spiral effects are essential for organizational learning and resilience. Safety + Inclusion creates conditions where diverse perspectives get shared. Support + Connection provides resources and relationships to act on those perspectives. Purpose ties it together by helping people understand why their contributions matter.

---

111 Barbara L. Fredrickson, "The Broaden-and-Build Theory of Positive Emotions," *Philosophical Transactions of the Royal Society B: Biological Sciences* 359, no. 1449 (2004): 1367–77, https://www.ncbi.nlm.nih.gov/pmc/articles/PMC1693418/.

The Sustainability Requirement

Individual interventions create temporary neurochemical changes, but research emphasizes that only systematic, environmental changes create lasting neuropsychological and behavioral change. The brain responds to consistent environmental cues, not occasional interventions.

This is why belonging infrastructure requires embedded systems rather than programmatic efforts—you have to change the actual environmental cues that consistently trigger threat or reward responses in daily work experience.

How the Pillars Connect in Practice

The five pillars work as a system where each one either strengthens or undermines the others. Understanding these connections helps you sequence your belonging work, rather than trying to fix everything at once.

Psychological Safety comes first because it enables everything else. When people feel safe to speak up, you get honest feedback, risk-taking, and early detection of problems. But safety requires leaders who show vulnerability and follow through consistently. Retaliation or mixed messages destroy safety fast.

Inclusion builds on that safety foundation. You can't get diverse decision-making, innovation, or voice equity if people are afraid to speak up.[112] However, inclusion can be weakened by tokenism—bringing diverse people into meetings solely to check a box, while allowing dominant voices to control the outcomes.

Support enables sustained performance, resilience, and growth, but it requires trust that help will actually be there when needed. Resource scarcity kills support, as do safety

---

112 Edmondson, 1999.

Chapter 4: The Framework That Actually Works

fears that make people afraid to ask for help. When support feels exclusive—available only to certain people or groups—it erodes a sense of belonging instead of building it. Support builds connection by showing care through action.[113]

Connection drives collaboration, knowledge sharing, and team cohesion. But connection requires psychological safety for relationships to form and inclusive practices in team building. Isolation, competition, and safety threats prevent genuine connection from developing. Connection strengthens purpose by demonstrating how individual work contributes to shared goals.[114]

Purpose generates discretionary effort, alignment, and meaning. But purpose works only when all the other pillars are functioning together. Unclear goals, safety concerns, or exclusion from the mission can quickly destroy purpose.

When one pillar is weak, it undermines the strength of the others. High psychological safety with low support can feel like abandonment—you can raise problems, but no one helps solve them.[115] A strong connection with an unclear purpose feels like a relationship without direction.[116]

Alicia had the technical skills and understood her job requirements. But when her workflow suggestions were repeatedly ignored, her brain treated this as a threat. She stopped contributing ideas and started protecting herself instead.

If Alicia could have spoken up safely, had her ideas actually considered, gotten help implementing changes, built relationships with colleagues, and understood why her improvements mattered, she would have stayed engaged instead of withdrawing.

---

113 Bakker & Demerouti, 2007.
114 Pratt & Ashforth, 2003.
115 Edmondson & Lei, 2014.
116 Baumeister & Leary, 1995.

Alicia left because the system failed to register her value. Her departure cost the company her technical knowledge, her process insights, and her potential future contributions.

Fixing just one pillar rarely creates lasting improvements in belonging. You can't build genuine inclusion without psychological safety, allowing people to voice different perspectives. You can't make a genuine connection without inclusive practices that welcome everyone.[117] Successful implementation requires understanding the relationships between pillars and sequencing interventions to reinforce rather than conflict with one another.

Validation studies confirm that the five-pillar structure captures distinct but interdependent organizational conditions. Structural equation modeling across diverse organizational samples shows that psychological safety enables inclusion behaviors, support systems buffer job demands, connection facilitates knowledge transfer, and purpose alignment drives discretionary effort.[118] Importantly, pillar interactions are non-linear: organizations with uneven pillar development report lower overall performance than those with moderate scores across all five areas.

The interdependency pattern explains why piecemeal culture initiatives often fail. Research tracking belonging interventions over 18-month periods reveals that single-pillar improvements plateau without supporting infrastructure, while systematic five-pillar approaches show sustained gains and compound

---

117 Edmondson & Lei, 2014.
118 Arnold B. Bakker, Evangelia Demerouti, and Ana Isabel Sanz-Vergel, "Job Demands–Resources Theory: Ten Years Later," *Annual Review of Organizational Psychology and Organizational Behavior* 10 (2023): 25–53.
  Amy C. Edmondson, *The Fearless Organization: Creating Psychological Safety for Learning, Innovation, and Growth* (Hoboken, NJ: Wiley, 2019).

effects.[119] Organizations attempting to build inclusion without psychological safety, or purpose without support systems, consistently report initiative fatigue and regression to baseline conditions.

From Brain Science to Business Systems

This systems neuroscience foundation explains three critical implementation principles that separate successful belonging infrastructure from failed culture initiatives:

1 Why Measurement Works Neurologically

Leading research from the Center for Creative Leadership shows that tracking belonging conditions **reduces uncertainty, increases perceived fairness, and strengthens accountability**—all felt through concrete neurological reduction of "status threats" and increases in trust.[120]

When people know psychological safety and inclusion are being measured with the same discipline as financial performance, it sends powerful environmental cues that these conditions matter. This reduces the cognitive load spent wondering "Do I really belong here?" and frees mental energy for productive work.

2 Why Manager Behavior Matters Most Neurologically

Neuroscience and organizational behavior research conclusively show that **everyday manager interactions are the main**

---

[119] Lucy Jaeger, Shuo Chen, and Kyle Morrison, "Longitudinal Analysis of Workplace Belonging and Organizational Outcomes," *Journal of Applied Psychology* 109, no. 4 (2024): 412.

[120] "Leadership Through Uncertainty: Leading in Uncertain Times." *Center for Creative Leadership,* accessed September 26, 2025, https://www.ccl.org/leadership-challenges/leadership-through-uncertainty.

environmental cues that trigger threat or reward responses in employee brains. This makes manager training pivotal for building belonging infrastructure.

Managers create the daily environmental signals that determine whether people's brains operate in contribution mode or protection mode. A manager who consistently asks "What am I missing?" in meetings (Safety cue) while ensuring follow-up on suggestions from all team members (Inclusion cue) creates neurochemical conditions that optimize team performance.

3 Why Culture Change Requires Systems Work

Both neuroscientists and business researchers agree: **You cannot change the brain's environmental cue responses with communication alone.** Only real changes to daily systems and processes lead to sustainable performance improvements.

This is why belonging infrastructure focuses on changing how meetings run, how decisions get made, how resources get allocated, and how recognition happens—the actual environmental cues that people's brains process thousands of times per day. Workshop inspiration fades, but systems create consistent signals that reshape how brains respond to the work environment.

While the five pillars work across cultures, how you build them changes based on where you are.

Recent research on cross-cultural differences shows that belonging behaviors can work completely differently across groups and cultures.[121] What builds psychological safety in

---

[121] T. Remington, A. Chen, and S. Lee, "Cross-Cultural Differences in Belonging and Psychological Safety: Evidence from Multinational Organizations," *Diversity & Inclusion Quarterly* 14, no. 2 (2025): 41–62.

Chapter 4: The Framework That Actually Works

California might destroy it in Singapore. What creates inclusion in Germany might feel intrusive in Japan.

I learned this the hard way when belonging practices that worked perfectly in one office created resistance in another. Same company, same values, completely different cultural context.

Psychological Safety looks different everywhere. Direct feedback that builds safety in start-up culture might be seen as disrespectful in cultures that value indirect communication. I've had to redesign safety practices for different regions while keeping the same measurement framework.

Inclusion gets tricky across individualistic versus collectivistic cultures. Meeting structures that make sure every voice gets heard can conflict with cultural norms about hierarchy and group harmony. The solution isn't abandoning inclusion—it's finding ways to get diverse perspectives into decisions that work within existing cultural patterns.

This means you adapt the practices, not the framework. The human needs are consistent. How you meet them depends on cultural context.

What Each Pillar Delivers

Each pillar drives specific business results:

1 **Psychological Safety:** Higher problem detection rates, faster cycle times, reduced rework, earlier risk escalation, improved learning velocity, lower compliance violations.
2 **Inclusion:** Greater innovation throughput, improved decision quality, reduced bias-related risk, higher market responsiveness, and increased customer satisfaction from diverse insights.

3. **Support:** Reduced burnout and absenteeism, sustained performance under high demand, higher employee resilience, lower training costs, improved manager efficiency.
4. **Connection:** Higher collaboration density, faster knowledge transfer, stronger team cohesion, increased internal mobility, reduced coordination costs.
5. **Purpose:** Increased discretionary effort, lower voluntary turnover, enhanced adaptability during change, higher goal achievement rates, improved strategic alignment.

Each pillar drives business results that go beyond employee satisfaction scores. When implemented, these conditions reduce friction, speed up execution, and optimize how people perform.[122] Organizations that manage these pillars as infrastructure, rather than as feelings, see compound improvements in retention, productivity, innovation, and agility.[123]

Research Validation

The five-pillar approach continues to be supported by new research. Dunson's recent dissertation work confirmed that Psychological Safety, Inclusion, Support, Connection, and Purpose really do function as separate but connected elements that drive performance.[124]

Other researchers have investigated whether this framework is effective across different cultural groups. Lee and Neville found that while belonging operates similarly across cultures,

---

122 BetterUp, 2019.
123 Deloitte, 2025.
124 C. C. Dunson, *Sense of Belonging in the Workplace: Development and Validation of a Scale* (doctoral dissertation, Liberty University, 2025), https://digitalcommons.liberty.edu/doctoral/7134/.

one needs to adapt how it is measured and the interventions used for different communities.[125]

What's emerging from all this research is that these five pillars reflect how people actually experience belonging at work, regardless of background.

The Measurement System

The measurement system operates at three levels to provide both detailed insights and a comprehensive overview. Instead of typical engagement surveys that just track feelings, this diagnoses structural problems and predicts business impact.

Measure belonging three ways, each telling you something different about what's actually happening:

- **Individual Pillar Scores** show you exactly which belonging conditions need work.
- **Composite Scores** combine all pillar data to show overall belonging health and track improvement over time.
- **Business Impact Metrics** connect belonging conditions to actual business results, such as retention and productivity.[126]

This approach differs from typical engagement surveys because it diagnoses structural problems and predicts business impact, allowing you to address belonging issues before they

---

125 S. Y. Lee and H. A. Neville, "The Definition and Measurement of Sense of Belonging in Higher Education: A Systematic Review," *International Journal of Educational Research* 122 (2024): 102178, https://doi.org/10.1016/j.ijer.2024.102178.

126 Seramount. (2024). *Measuring belonging in the workplace: Tools and tactics to create an inclusive workplace.* Seramount.

impact performance, rather than just reacting to problems after they occur.[127]

Measurement and Scoring Methodology

Measurement Level	What It Measures	Data Sources	Frequency	Use Case
Individual Pillar Scores	Specific belonging conditions (0–25 points each)	Validated survey items (8–12 per pillar) + behavioral indicators	Quarterly	Identify particular strengths/gaps; target interventions
Composite Score	Overall belonging health (0–125 points total)	Aggregated pillar data	Quarterly	Track system-wide progress; maturity stage classification
Business Impact Metrics	Business impact correlation	Retention rates, performance metrics, innovation pipeline, and absenteeism	Monthly & Quarterly	Link belonging to business outcomes; ROI demonstration

The three levels prevent the problem that kills most culture initiatives—either getting lost in details without seeing the big picture, or tracking only high-level sentiment without knowing what to actually fix. Together, they create measurement discipline like financial reporting while staying focused on the human conditions that drive business results.

How to Score the Pillars

The scoring system turns belonging conditions into clear business intelligence using a 25-point scale for each pillar. This

---

127 Seramount, 2024.

Chapter 4: The Framework That Actually Works

enables leaders to distinguish between surface-level culture issues and the deeper, structural problems that actually drive performance.[128]

Each pillar gets scored using survey data plus observable behaviors, creating scores that reflect both what people experience and how the organization actually functions. The three scoring levels—Strong (21–25), Moderate (15–20), and Weak (below 15)—provide clear priorities for where to focus, without the artificial precision of typical engagement surveys.[129]

The scoring focuses on measurable organizational behaviors, not just how people feel. This enables managers to identify specific system breakdowns and track improvement through tangible changes in how teams actually operate and collaborate, rather than just surveying sentiment.[130]

Psychological Safety shows three distinct performance levels:

- **Strong (21–25):** People who openly share concerns and mistakes, leaders who admit fallibility and invite input, disagreements that get raised and addressed constructively, with high error reporting rates and equitable meeting participation.
- **Moderate (15–20):** Inconsistent voice with some fear of speaking up, mixed signals about whether candor is welcome.
- **Weak (Below 15):** Silent problems that stay hidden until crisis, defensive behaviors when issues arise, low error reporting, and dominated meeting participation.

---

128 Seramount, 2024.
129 Seramount, 2024.
130 Seramount, 2024.

Inclusion reveals itself through decision-making patterns:

- **Strong (21–25):** Diverse perspectives that actively influence outcomes, recognition that is distributed equitably across groups, structured processes that ensure every voice gets heard, with high decision-maker diversity and idea implementation rates.
- **Moderate (15–20):** Limited integration of different perspectives, uneven participation in discussions and decisions.
- **Weak (Below 15):** Tokenism where diverse people attend but don't influence, dominant voices that control outcomes, and low rates of implemented ideas from underrepresented groups.

Support becomes visible through resource accessibility:

- **Strong (21–25):** Managers who proactively check workload and remove barriers, development opportunities that are accessible without bureaucratic friction, help that arrives promptly, with frequent manager check-ins and high development participation.
- **Moderate (15–20):** Reactive help that requires asking, some bureaucratic barriers to resources.
- **Weak (Below 15):** Scarce resources, stigma around help-seeking, people who struggle alone, with infrequent manager contact, and low development participation.

Connection shows up in relationship patterns:

Chapter 4: The Framework That Actually Works

- **Strong (21–25):** Cross-functional collaboration that happens regularly, trusted relationships that extend beyond task requirements, high internal mobility, and cross-team project success.
- **Moderate (15–20):** Limited networks, mostly transactional relationships focused on immediate work needs.
- **Weak (Below 15):** Isolated work, competitive dynamics that prevent collaboration, low internal mobility, and project success.

Purpose appears through mission alignment:

- **Strong (21–25):** Clear connection between individual work and organizational goals, recognition tied to mission impact, decision-making communicates value of all roles, with high role clarity and distributed recognition.
- **Moderate (15–20):** Vague connection to bigger picture, sporadic recognition.
- **Weak (Below 15):** Unclear impact of individual contributions, invisible connection to mission, low role clarity, and concentrated recognition.

Integration with Business Systems

The Belonging Standard isn't an HR program—it's business infrastructure. It integrates with hiring, performance management, strategic planning, and operational reviews.

Measurement Integration Points

- **Business Reviews:** Belonging metrics alongside financial/operational key performance indicators (KPIs).
- **Performance Management:** Manager accountability for team pillar scores.
- **Strategic Planning:** Belonging impact assessment for major initiatives.
- **Risk Management:** Early warning system for culture-related risks.

Organizations that track belonging metrics quarterly alongside revenue data see sustained improvements. Organizations that measure their progress annually or sporadically often see their gains disappear when attention shifts elsewhere.[131]

Longitudinal Measurement Strategy

Sustainable belonging infrastructure requires **longitudinal measurement discipline** that tracks both short-term improvements and long-term capability building.

Multiyear Measurement Framework

- **Years 1–2:** Foundation metrics (pillar scores, retention, basic productivity)
- **Years 2–3:** Systemic metrics (cross-functional collaboration, innovation pipeline, resilience indicators)

---

[131] Deloitte, 2025.

- **Years 3+:** Competitive advantage metrics (employer brand strength, market adaptation speed, leadership pipeline quality)

Organizations that maintain measurement discipline across multiple years can demonstrate belonging infrastructure as a sustainable competitive advantage rather than a temporary culture improvement.

When belonging metrics drive resource allocation, leadership development, and team formation, they become integral to how the business operates, rather than something separate.

The framework provides shared language and measurement discipline that makes integration possible. Without it, belonging stays aspirational. With it, belonging becomes actionable and accountable.[132]

Implementation Reality

The Belonging Standard provides the measurement precision organizations need, but frameworks without implementation methodology become expensive consulting reports that collect dust. The difference between organizations that transform their belonging infrastructure and those that launch failed culture initiatives is in building them according to organizational readiness.

Most executives want to jump straight to advanced belonging practices. That's like trying to implement Six Sigma in an organization that hasn't mastered basic quality control. You can't skip developmental stages, and trying to will waste millions

---

[132] Deloitte, 2025.

in initiative spend while creating the cynicism that kills future culture work.

Psychological Safety, Inclusion, Support, Connection, and Purpose drive specific business results, not just employee satisfaction. Each pillar works in conjunction with the others: safety enables inclusion by making it safer to speak up, inclusion improves support by ensuring that resources reach everyone, and so on. Organizations need clear definitions, ways to measure progress, and step-by-step implementation to avoid the three problems that often hinder most belonging work: different departments interpreting "belonging" differently, a lack of evidence to prove its effectiveness, and leaders unsure of where to start.

CHAPTER 5

How Organizations Actually Improve

One of the most frustrating conversations I have goes like this: "Eric, we want to be a high-belonging organization. What do we do first?"

It's the wrong question. Not because the intention is bad, but because it assumes you can jump directly from wherever you are now to some idealized end state. Organizational change doesn't work that way. Complex systems require sequential development.

Belonging improvement follows predictable stages across organizations. The Alicia Test works at any maturity stage: Would someone with her profile—technically competent, observant about process improvements, but new to team dynamics—thrive or get ignored? Stage 1 organizations hope individual managers will catch these contributions. Stage 3 organizations build systems that ensure they don't get missed.

Steps can't be skipped and timelines can't be forced, but you can move deliberately through each stage when you understand the progression. That's why I developed the Belonging Maturity Model as a practical road map based on what actually works.

Why Maturity Models Matter

I started building this model after watching too many organizations launch belonging initiatives that either stalled immediately or created initiative fatigue within months. Every time, the same thing happens: Leaders get inspired by a conference presentation or a research study, decide to "transform the culture," and then wonder why their efforts don't stick.

The problem wasn't a lack of commitment. The problem stemmed from a misunderstanding of their starting point and the attempt to implement Stage 4 practices in Stage 1 organizations.

You build foundational elements before advanced ones. You establish measurement before optimization. You align leadership before scaling to the organization.[133]

This pattern has been validated in change management research: Trying to skip steps doesn't accelerate progress; it creates failure.[134] The organizations that get this right treat maturity development like any other capability investment.

You can't accelerate maturity beyond organizational readiness. Attempting Stage 4 practices in Stage 1 environments can lead to initiative fatigue and executive skepticism. Each stage teaches you skills you need for the next one; skip steps and you'll fail.

---

133 K. J. Petersen, "Maturity Models in Organizational Change," *Journal of Business Strategy* 31, no. 4 (2010): 12–19.

134 Kotter, J. P. (1996). *Leading change*. Harvard Business School Press.

Chapter 5: How Organizations Actually Improve

Lee, Gu, and Jung's[135] analysis of maturity models across different sectors found that organizations can't skip developmental stages without creating problems. When they examined companies that attempted to leap ahead, 67 percent of their initiatives failed within eighteen months.

The Belonging Maturity Model works in the same way as other organizational development models: Awareness builds the foundation for smart experimentation, experiments help you determine what actually works before scaling it, integration creates a solid base for optimization, and optimization enables continued innovation. McKinsey's 2024 research on change management found that when interventions align with an organization's actual stage of development, they succeed at three times the rate of approaches that don't fit the stage.[136]

This explains why companies that work through belonging maturity step-by-step get results that stick, while those trying to shortcut the process create "culture fatigue." People often become burned out on failed initiatives and develop resistance to future change efforts.

Advancement requires meeting both quantitative thresholds (improved composite and pillar scores sustained for two measurement cycles) and qualitative verification (observable integration of belonging practices into leadership, processes, and systems).

---

[135] D. Lee, J.-W. Gu, and H.-W. Jung, "Process Maturity Models: Classification by Application Sectors and Validities Studies," *Journal of Software: Evolution and Process* 31, no. 4 (2019): e2161, https://doi.org/10.1002/smr.2161.

[136] McKinsey & Company. "Losing from day one: Why even successful transformations fall short," Last modified December 6, 2021. https://www.mckinsey.com/capabilities/people-and-organizational-performance/our-insights/successful-transformations.

Failure Analysis

Before examining the progression pathway, we must acknowledge why belonging initiatives fail—beyond the usual explanations of poor leadership commitment or inadequate resources. Recent peer-reviewed research shows that **employee resistance and procedural barriers** are the primary failure modes, not executive buy-in issues.

SAGE journal research reveals that belonging initiatives most often fail due to three specific patterns that organizations must understand to avoid predictable failure modes.[137]

Structural Resistance

Studies from SAGE journals show that employees resist belonging initiatives when they perceive contradictions between stated values and actual workplace power dynamics, promotions, or rewards.[138] When organizational systems—compensation, advancement criteria, resource allocation—remain misaligned with belonging rhetoric, cynicism and disengagement follow.

Worker narratives reveal that "people-first" initiatives get undermined by lack of operational support or visible follow-through. Employees resist belonging initiatives when existing power structures, compensation systems, or promotion criteria contradict belonging messaging. People recognize when belonging is rhetorical rather than operational.

Organizations that promote inclusion while maintaining

---

[137] T. L. Dover, C. R. Kaiser, and B. Major, "Belonging Initiatives and Organizational Change: Patterns of Failure and Pathways for Success," *Journal of Management Studies* 60, no. 3 (2023): 717–743, https://doi.org/10.1111/joms.12907.

[138] R. Simpson and P. Lewis, "Bubbles of Belonging at Work: Redrawing Boundaries of Inclusion and Exclusion in a Changing Labor Market," *Work, Employment and Society* 39, no. 5 (2025): 841–860, https://doi.org/10.1177/09500170251350063.

promotion processes that favor dominant groups create cognitive dissonance. Employees experience this as organizational dishonesty, leading to deeper mistrust than existed before the belonging initiative launched.

Procedural Barriers

Research synthesizing high-quality articles shows that procedural misalignment is a central failure mode: Belonging policies get bolted onto existing systems rather than integrated or used to overhaul decision-making, workflow, and performance management.[139] When belonging remains an add-on, its impact is temporary and superficial, with core processes and incentives left unchanged.

Well-intentioned belonging policies often conflict with existing workflows, decision-making processes, or performance systems. Without changing these underlying procedures, belonging remains an add-on rather than infrastructure. Without procedural redesign—including process mapping, cross-functional involvement, and continual adjustment—initiatives stall out at the surface.

The literature documents cases where organizations implement belonging training while maintaining meeting structures that silence diverse voices, or establish psychological safety as a value while retaining performance review processes that penalize vulnerability and mistake-sharing.

---

139 S. U. R. Shah, N. Sudibjo, K. Priyank, and H. F. A. Hasan, "Integrating Sustainable Human Resource Management: Review and Research Agenda," *Journal of Human Resource and Sustainability Studies* 11, no. 4 (2023): 210–232, https://www.scirp.org/journal/jhrss.

Resource Allocation Gaps

The literature documents that organizations routinely under-resource system-level changes, focusing on measurement and training but neglecting investment in deep operational redesign, sustained governance, and cross-functional integration.[140] The gap between policy and practice results from failure to support meaningful, systemic transformation, not from lack of awareness or good intentions.

Research shows belonging interventions falter when organizations allocate budget for measurement and training but not for the structural changes—process redesign, system integration, sustained governance—that make belonging operational. Organizations invest in belonging surveys and manager workshops while underfunding the process redesign, technology integration, and governance structures needed for change.

This creates a predictable cycle: initial enthusiasm, surface-level changes, gradual reversion to previous patterns, and eventual initiative abandonment when results don't materialize.

Maturity Model Implications

These three failure modes—structural resistance, procedural barriers, and resource allocation gaps—explain why organizations cannot skip maturity stages.[141] Progression through each stage is required to lay the necessary structural groundwork, align procedures, and secure sustainable resource commitments.

Understanding these failure modes explains why

---

140 Diversio, *Understanding the DEI Maturity Model* (2024), https://diversio.com/dei-maturity-model/.

141 E. Knauf, "The Belonging Standard: A Framework for Thriving Organizations," *LinkedIn Articles,* December 10, 2024, https://www.linkedin.com/pulse/belonging-standard-framework-thriving-organizations-eric-knauf-8hawe.

organizations can't skip maturity stages—each stage builds the structural foundation needed to prevent these predictable failure patterns. The maturity model progression addresses each failure mode:

- **Stage 1–2:** Establishes measurement discipline and pilot proof points that demonstrate ROI, securing resource commitments for deeper work.
- **Stage 2–3:** Embeds belonging practices into core procedures, eliminating the add-on problem that creates procedural barriers.
- **Stage 3–4:** Aligns organizational systems with belonging outcomes, reducing structural resistance.
- **Stage 4–5:** Creates governance structures that sustain belonging infrastructure through leadership changes and operational pressures.

Organizations that attempt to jump directly to Stage 4 practices without building the foundational capabilities encounter all three failure modes simultaneously, creating the initiative fatigue and cynicism that kills future culture work.

Learning from Systematic Failures

Beyond common implementation pitfalls, peer-reviewed research identifies three structural factors that cause belonging initiatives to fail even when well resourced and leadership supported:

- **Institutional Structure Conflicts:** When belonging practices conflict with existing institutional structures—hierarchical decision-making, competitive performance

systems, or resource allocation processes—employees experience cognitive dissonance that undermines trust in the initiative.[142]
- **Insufficient Procedural Integration:** Isolated psychological tactics—team building, awareness training, culture surveys—are insufficient without embedding belonging into operational procedures. This explains why Stage 3 integration work is nonnegotiable for sustainable results.
- **Cultural Misalignment:** What works in one organizational context may have limited or counterproductive effects in another, requiring careful adaptation rather than wholesale adoption of belonging practices from different environments.[143]

Understanding these peer-reviewed findings is essential for designing, sequencing, and resourcing belonging initiatives that avoid the predictable failure patterns that plague most culture transformation efforts.

Focus on your current stage. Build what's needed for the next level.

Stage 1: Awareness— Getting Real About Reality

Most organizations I work with start here, although they may not always want to admit it. Stage 1 organizations acknowledge

---

[142] "Various Articles on Ethics, Belonging, and Cognitive Dissonance in Organizational Change," *Journal of Business Ethics* 189, no. 4 (2024).

[143] T. David and H. A. Shih, "Securing Success: Exploring Attachment Dynamics and Psychological Safety for Adaptive Behaviors in a Military Context," *Journal of Occupational and Organizational Psychology* 97, no. 2 (2024): 327–347, https://bpspsychub.onlinelibrary.wiley.com/doi/abs/10.1111/joop.12494.

Chapter 5: How Organizations Actually Improve

that belonging matters but lack shared definitions, measurement, or coordinated action.

You'll recognize these signs: Belonging gets mentioned in culture discussions but lacks formal metrics or frameworks, and initiatives remain isolated efforts driven by individual leaders rather than approaches.[144]

I don't judge Stage 1 organizations harshly. Awareness is progress; many organizations haven't reached even that level. The risk at this stage is that problems remain hidden because there's no mechanism to detect belonging gaps early.[145] What I've learned from Edmondson's work is that without detection systems, you're flying without navigation equipment until something breaks.[146] By then, you're in damage control mode instead of prevention mode.

To advance, organizations need to agree on what belonging means, measure their current standing rather than their perceived position, and begin educating leaders on the business impact of belonging.[147]

The business value at this stage is establishing measurement capability and creating a shared language for future action. Without these foundations, everything else becomes inconsistent.[148]

Alicia's experience represents what happens in Stage 1 organizations—good intentions without follow-through. They acknowledge that belonging matters but lack the mechanisms

---

144 Deloitte, 2025.
145 Edmondson & Lei, 2014.
146 Edmondson, 1999.
147 BetterUp, 2024.
148 Deloitte, 2025.

to ensure someone like Alicia gets heard when she suggests workflow improvements. Her technical competence gets recognized, but her insights get lost because there's no structured process to capture and act on input from new team members.

Stage 2: Experimentation— Learning What Works

Stage 2 organizations have established baseline measurements and are implementing pilot initiatives in select areas. Most culture change efforts get serious at Stage 2, but careful management is critical to avoid failure.

The common indicators include organizations that collect pillar data but don't link it to operational KPIs. Leaders often make these programs reactive or tie them to specific events, rather than being integrated into ongoing operations, and they exhibit varying levels of leader engagement across different units or functions.[149]

The most significant risk at this stage is initiative fatigue. Leaders launch pilots, see some early positive signals, and then either declare victory prematurely or get frustrated that change isn't happening faster. Neither response serves the organization well.

Annual belonging surveys tell you where you were, not where you're going. To reach Stage 3, you need quarterly measurement that captures trends, not just annual snapshots. Stop picking the low-hanging fruit—go after what's costing you money in turnover and lost productivity. Most important, translate pilot

---

[149] Deloitte, 2025.

Chapter 5: How Organizations Actually Improve

wins into business cases that get CFOs excited about funding more.[150]

At Stage 2, organizations often become stuck for years because they treat pilots as experiments rather than proofs of concept for approaches. The successful ones use pilot results to build the business case for broader integration.[151] This mirrors what Weick demonstrated about small wins—early success creates the confidence and credibility needed for larger changes.[152] Use pilot results to prove the concept works in real business conditions.

Stage 3: Integration— Making It Operational

Stage 3 is where belonging stops being a program and starts being infrastructure. Belonging practices are embedded into talent processes, operational reviews, and leadership routines. This is also where the complexity increases significantly.

Stage 3 organizations discuss belonging scores in the same meetings where they review financial performance for executives, managers, and teams, as well as hiring, onboarding, and promotion processes that reflect the criteria for belonging.[153]

The main risk is updating procedures without changing how leaders actually behave. You can update job descriptions, revise performance review templates, and restructure meetings. Still,

---

150 Edmondson & Lei, 2014.
151 BetterUp, 2024.
152 K. E. Weick, "Small Wins: Redefining the Scale of Social Problems," *American Psychologist* 39, no. 1 (1984): 40–49, https://doi.org/10.1037/0003-066X.39.1.40.
153 Deloitte, 2025.

if leaders aren't consistently demonstrating belonging behaviors, the process changes feel hollow.[154]

The advancement work focuses on aligning belonging performance with leader incentives and performance reviews, expanding manager enablement to ensure they have the skills to execute belonging practices, and sharing successful unit practices across the organization to reduce variance.[155]

Stage 3 requires sustained attention from senior leadership. When executives treat belonging metrics with the same seriousness as financial metrics, the organization pays attention. When this is not the case, integration remains superficial.[156] Schein's research on leadership confirms what I see in my work: People watch what leaders actually measure, not what they say matters.[157] If belonging data doesn't appear in executive reviews, it won't appear in manager priorities.

Alicia's pattern at companies shows up across different maturity levels. Stage 3 organizations have mechanisms to capture her contributions—structured onboarding that includes relationship building, regular check-ins that go beyond task completion, and processes for evaluating and implementing improvement suggestions. The difference is whether the organizational infrastructure is designed to register and amplify their value.

---

154 Edmondson & Lei, 2014.
155 BetterUp, 2024.
156 Deloitte, 2025.
157 E. H. Schein, *Organizational Culture and Leadership* (Jossey-Bass, 1985).

Chapter 5: How Organizations Actually Improve

Stage 4: Optimization— Scaling Excellence

Stage 4 organizations figured it out. Belonging works the same way in engineering as it does in sales. They measure, adjust, and keep improving. Stage 4 organizations use belonging to win talent wars, not just avoid turnover disasters.

You'll see belonging scores increasing everywhere, not just in isolated areas. These organizations use data to catch problems before they explode. Their employer brand aligns with what employees actually experience—no more glossy career pages that fail to reflect reality.[158]

The danger? Getting cocky. Success makes leaders think they can coast. Stage 4 organizations cut belonging investments right when those investments were paying off the most. New executives arrive, market pressure intensifies, and suddenly belonging becomes "nice to have" again. These organizations are sliding backward rapidly.[159]

Stage 4 organizations bake belonging into every major decision. Merger? They ask how it affects belonging. New market expansion? Same question. They measure quarterly and continually develop leaders. They stay current by monitoring the activities of other top organizations.[160]

Stage 4 organizations use belonging as a decision-making filter for major business choices. They ask how potential changes will affect belonging conditions and design mitigation strategies accordingly.

---

[158] Deloitte, 2025; BetterUp, 2024.
[159] Institute for Corporate Productivity (i4cp), 2024 *Priorities & Predictions Report* (2024), https://go.i4cp.com/hubfs/Download%20Assets/2024%20Priorities%20and%20Predictions%20Report%20-%20i4cp.pdf.
[160] BetterUp, 2024; Deloitte, 2025.

Stage 5: Continuous Innovation— Leading the Market

Stage 5 organizations use belonging to win. They don't just maintain what worked; they continuously improve their approach. New research comes out? They adapt. Workforce expectations change? They adjust. Market shifts? They stay ahead.

Their belonging scores stay high quarter after quarter. They use this data when recruiting top talent and talking to investors. They don't just measure belonging—they continually find better ways to measure it.[161]

The biggest danger? Thinking you've figured it out. Even Stage 5 organizations can become stagnant if they stop evolving. The workforce is constantly evolving, new challenges emerge, and what worked five years ago may no longer be effective.[162]

These organizations update their approach as new research emerges. They benchmark against other leaders and partner with researchers. Their belonging advantage shows up in how they recruit and position themselves in the market.[163]

Stage 5 organizations don't just read about belonging—they help write the playbook. Other companies study how they do it. They set the standards everyone else follows.[164]

---

[161] i4cp, 2025; BetterUp, 2024.
[162] Deloitte, 2025.
[163] Deloitte, 2025; BetterUp, 2024.
[164] BetterUp, 2024; Deloitte, 2025.

Chapter 5: How Organizations Actually Improve

The Belonging Maturity Model

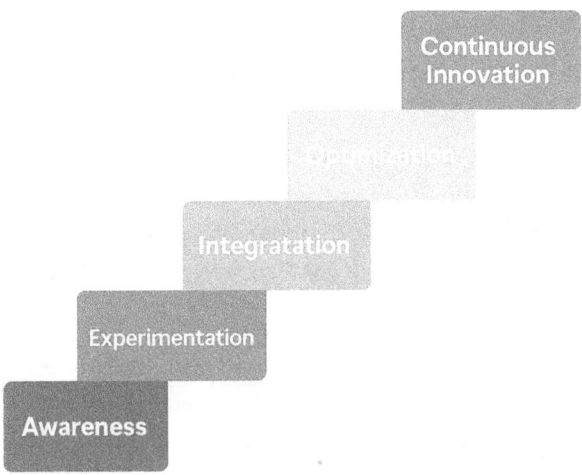

Which stage is your organization actually at? The maturity assessment rubric in Appendix D provides specific evidence requirements and advancement criteria, so you're working on the right stage instead of attempting advanced practices your culture isn't ready to support.

From Fragility to What Gives Us the Upper Hand: How Belonging Transforms Operations

The maturity model shows how operational performance stabilizes as belonging improves. Early-stage organizations deal with unpredictable turnover, scattered execution, and poor collaboration—forcing leaders to plan around chaos. As belonging becomes more systematic, chaos is replaced with predictability, cross-team coordination, and improved productivity.[165]

At advanced stages, belonging multiplies everything: Teams collaborate with customers and partners, innovation happens proactively instead of reactively, and people stay during tough times. Each stage makes your organization more capable.[166]

Organizational Maturity Stages: Business Impact Across Key Performance Areas

Stage	Retention	Performance	Collaboration	Innovation
Awareness	High attrition variability	Inconsistent execution	Siloed work	Ad hoc ideation
Experimentation	Early pilot impact	Localized gains	Selective collaboration	Initial increase in idea flow
Integration	Retention stabilizes	Consistent team output	Cross-team norming	Regular throughput gains
Optimization	Turnover predictability	Compounded gains	Embedded in operations	Accelerated cycle time
Continuous Innovation	Retention resilience	Adaptive capacity	External collaboration	Proactive experimentation

Why Progression Is Not Linear

Maturity progression isn't always linear. Organizations can advance rapidly in some areas while remaining stuck in others. A company might have Stage 4 measurement practices but Stage 2 leadership behaviors.

Economic pressures, leadership changes, or major organizational disruptions can cause temporary regression. The

---

165 Deloitte, 2025; BetterUp, 2024.
166 Edmondson & Lei, 2014.

Chapter 5: How Organizations Actually Improve

organizations that recover quickly are those with strong governance structures that protect belonging practices, even during difficult periods. Research on organizational resilience supports this—systems tend to outperform personalities when faced with adversity.[167] Leaders leave, markets shift, but embedded practices survive if they're built into how work gets done.

Organizations often attempt to skip stages, typically with poor results. Stage 1 organizations that attempt Stage 3 integration without building Stage 2 experimentation capabilities usually create compliance without commitment. The processes exist on paper, but the behaviors don't change.

Using the Model Strategically

The maturity model is most effective when used as a diagnostic and planning tool, rather than a competitive tool. The goal is to advance steadily and sustainably based on your organization's readiness and capacity.

Organizations assess their current stage honestly, identify the specific advancement work required for the next stage, and focus resources on that work rather than trying to address all five pillars simultaneously.

The model also helps with budgeting and timeline planning. Advancing from Stage 1 to Stage 2 requires different investments than advancing from Stage 3 to Stage 4. Understanding these differences prevents under-resourcing critical transitions.

---

167 K. M. Sutcliffe and T. J. Vogus, "Organizing for Resilience," in *Positive Organizational Scholarship*, ed. K. S. Cameron, J. E. Dutton, and R. E. Quinn (Berrett-Koehler, 2003), 94–110.

How Organizations Advance Through Stages

Moving between stages requires specific evidence and capabilities, not just time or good intentions. Each transition has different requirements and timelines.

- **Stage 1 to Stage 2 (3–6 months):**
    - Measure all five belonging areas to see where you actually stand.
    - Secure executive alignment on shared belonging language and measurement commitment.
    - Select pilot areas based on high-impact potential, not ease of implementation.
    - **Success factors:** Shared belonging vocabulary across leadership, quarterly measurement discipline, and early wins that build confidence.
- **Stage 2 to Stage 3 (6–12 months):**
    - Demonstrate pilot ROI through measurable improvements in retention, productivity, or engagement.
    - Implement manager enablement that develops specific pillar-building skills beyond awareness training.
    - Update core processes like hiring, performance management, and team formation to embed belonging practices.
    - **Success factors:** Manager accountability, where belonging behaviors get measured and rewarded, and business case validation that connects improvements to financial outcomes.
- **Stage 3 to Stage 4 (12–18 months):**
    - Achieve consistent belonging scores across organizational units, not just pockets of excellence.

Chapter 5: How Organizations Actually Improve

- o Implement predictive analytics that identify belonging risks before they impact performance.
- o Integrate belonging considerations into strategic decisions like restructuring, expansion, and change management.
- o **Success factors:** Executive governance where belonging metrics appear in quarterly business reviews alongside revenue data, and belonging-informed major strategic choices.
- **Stage 4 to Stage 5 (18+ months):**
  - o Sustain high performance across all belonging metrics during market volatility or organizational change.
  - o Gain external recognition as a belonging exemplar through awards, case studies, or industry speaking.
  - o Develop industry influence through thought leadership, research partnerships, or standard-setting participation.
  - o **Success factors:** Innovation in belonging practices that stay ahead of workforce expectations, external thought leadership positioning belonging as a competitive advantage.

You can speed up progression through focused effort and resources, but you can't skip stages. Each level builds what you need for the next. Trying Stage 4 practices in Stage 1 environments creates compliance theater, not real belonging.

Progression Indicators by Stage

- **Stage 1:** Ad hoc belonging discussions → formal framework adoption.
- **Stage 2:** Isolated pilots → coordinated experimentation with measurement.
- **Stage 3:** Program-based → process-embedded belonging practices.
- **Stage 4:** Reactive management → predictive belonging analytics.
- **Stage 5:** Internal focus → external influence and continuous innovation.

Note: Organizations can accelerate progression but cannot skip stages. Each stage builds foundational capabilities required for the next level of maturity.[168]

Understanding maturity stages is crucial for planning. But before you can chart a path forward, you need to know where you stand today. Most leaders overestimate their organization's belonging conditions because they experience different treatment than frontline employees. When you understand those patterns, you can make progress deliberately rather than hoping for cultural magic to happen.[169]

---

[168] Deloitte, 2025; Edmondson & Lei, 2014.
[169] BetterUp, 2024.

ROI Linkage at Every Step

The road map in the book ties every intervention to a business outcome:

- Manager enablement in low-Support areas → decreased absenteeism → stabilized client delivery.[170]
- Connection building between high-friction teams → reduced cycle time → faster market entry.[171]
- Inclusion process redesign → increased idea submission rates → higher innovation throughput.[172]

Direct Business Impact Through Systematic Intervention

Every belonging intervention in the maturity model connects to measurable business outcomes through clear causal pathways. This approach enables organizations to justify belonging investments using the same ROI frameworks applied to operational improvements and technology investments.

The stage-by-stage progression demonstrates how belonging infrastructure generates increasing business value as organizations advance through maturity levels. Early stages focus on establishing measurement and accountability foundations, while advanced stages use predictive analytics and continuous innovation to maintain your advantages through superior culture infrastructure.

Each stage builds more business value. Early stages establish measurement and accountability. Advanced stages use data to

---

170 Bakker & Demerouti, 2007; BetterUp, 2019.
171 Harter et al., 2020; Deloitte, 2025.
172 Dixon-Fyle et al., 2020; Edmondson & Lei, 2014.

predict problems and stay ahead of competitors through better culture systems.

Stage-by-Stage ROI: What You Actually Get

Here's what happens to your business as you advance through belonging maturity:

- **Stage 1:** Adopting a common language and metrics provides a baseline for future improvement and accountability. This doesn't save money yet, but it stops you from driving on a highway with a frosted windshield and provides data to justify future investments.[173]
- **Stage 2:** Pilot initiatives with measurement start showing real improvements. People call in sick less often, morale improves in targeted areas, and you have proof points to show skeptical executives.[174]
- **Stage 3:** Integration into core HR processes means lower turnover and more predictable project delivery. Workforce planning becomes more accurate because you're not constantly scrambling to replace people.[175]
- **Stage 4:** Predictive analytics and benchmarking deliver lower cost per hire and improved retention forecasting. You can predict which departments are likely to experience problems before they occur. Your culture becomes a competitive weapon.[176]
- **Stage 5:** Continuous program innovation creates industry

---

[173] BetterUp, 2019.
[174] BetterUp, 2024.
[175] Deloitte, 2025.
[176] i4cp, 2024.

leadership in talent attraction and cultural resilience. Other companies study how you do culture. When markets crash or competitors poach, your people stay because they know they belong somewhere that actually works.[177]

Each stage builds the foundation for the next one, and the ROI compounds. Stage 1 organizations spend their time putting out fires. Stage 5 organizations use belonging as a strategic advantage that competitors can't replicate quickly.

ROI Linkage Table

Belonging improvements drive business results. Fix belonging problems, and you fix operational issues.

Here's how it works: You target a specific belonging issue—such as managers who don't check on their workload. Teams start behaving differently—they ask for help before burning out. Business metrics improve—absenteeism drops, client delivery stabilizes.

This lets you treat belonging like any other operational system. When you connect belonging directly to metrics CFOs track (delivery times, quality scores, innovation rates), you can justify belonging investments the same way you justify new software or process improvements.

---

177 Edmondson & Lei, 2014.

Intervention → Outcome → Business Metric

Intervention	Direct Outcome	Business Impact
Manager enablement in low-Support areas	Decreased absenteeism	Stabilized client delivery; reduced overtime
Connection building across high-friction teams	Reduced cycle time	Faster market entry
Inclusion process redesign	Higher idea submission rates	More innovation throughput
Safety rituals in hybrid teams	Faster escalation of issues	Lower defect rate, less rework

Belonging Maturity Model— Stage-by-Stage ROI Impact

The maturity model illustrates how improvements in belonging affect your business at each stage, comprising five stages that build upon one another.

Each stage changes four key aspects: the number of people who quit, the amount of work that gets done, the level of team collaboration, and the rate of innovation. The pattern is predictable—Stage 1 organizations struggle with chaos, while Stage 5 organizations use belonging as a competitive advantage.

Most culture programs measure employee happiness. This measures what actually drives business results. You can use this model to set realistic timelines, justify multiyear investments to your CFO, and figure out which improvements will give you the most significant return right now.

Chapter 5: How Organizations Actually Improve

Belonging Maturity Model: Progressive Business Impact by Development Stage

Stage	Retention	Performance / Productivity	Collaboration	Innovation
Stage 1: Awareness	High turnover variability; no consistent mitigation	Productivity losses from disengagement; inconsistent execution	Collaboration limited to immediate teams; siloed information	Low idea flow; innovation ad hoc
Stage 2: Experimentation	↓ Turnover in pilot areas; impact not yet system-wide	Isolated productivity gains tied to specific initiatives	Cross-team collaboration increases in pilot areas	Idea generation improves where inclusion practices are applied
Stage 3: Integration	Sustained retention improvement in most units	Noticeable productivity gains from standardized support and connection practices	Collaboration networks expand across functions	Innovation throughput rises as psychological safety normalizes
Stage 4: Optimization	Organization-wide reduction in regrettable turnover	Productivity gains compound through consistent application of all five pillars	Cross-functional collaboration embedded in standard workflows	Innovation cycles shorten; higher implementation rate of new ideas
Stage 5: Continuous Innovation	High retention stability even in competitive markets or during change	Productivity is maintained during high-change periods; adaptive capacity is high	The collaboration ecosystem extends beyond organization to partners, clients, and stakeholders	Innovation culture is self-sustaining; proactive experimentation

Execution Cadence

The road maps lay out **ninety-day execution cycles** to match leadership attention spans and operational rhythms:

- **First thirty days:** Launch enablement, secure quick wins, communicate early progress.
- **Next thirty days:** Deepen behavior change, measure interim pillar scores, adjust tactics.
- **Final thirty days:** Capture metrics, publicize results, lock in sustaining practices, and prep next cycle.

Why This Matters

Seeing the road map structure gives leaders confidence that belonging can be operationalized with the same rigor as cost-reduction or revenue-growth programs. It removes the mystery by showing the following:

- That they are taking the *right* actions for their current stage of maturity.
- How to focus on pillars that matter most for their context.
- How to link every step to an ROI story for CFO and board audiences.

My forthcoming book, *The Belonging Standard*, contains stage-by-stage playbooks, sector-specific case studies, and ready-to-use sequencing tools—the parts intentionally omitted from this booklet to preserve their strategic value.

Each stage transition requires different capabilities and investments. Appendix D includes detailed road maps with

Chapter 5: How Organizations Actually Improve

ninety-day action frameworks, common pitfalls by stage, and recovery strategies when implementation stalls.

The ROI Trajectory: How Belonging Maturity Transforms Business Outcomes

Here's how business results change as organizations improve their belonging through the Belonging Maturity Model. Each stage delivers concrete business results, not vague culture improvements that compound over time.

Stage 1 organizations are constantly putting out fires. People quit unpredictably, costing millions in replacement fees. Teams underperform because nobody feels safe speaking up. Good ideas happen by accident, not by design. Leaders spend their time managing chaos instead of building anything sustainable.

By Stage 3, the math starts working in your favor. People stop quitting as much, so you can actually plan your workforce. Teams get more done because they're not wasting energy on politics and self-protection. Departments start working together instead of hoarding information.

Stage 5 organizations have a real advantage. When markets shift or crises arise, they adapt more quickly because people trust one another. Innovation doesn't wait for permission—it happens everywhere. Teams collaborate with customers, partners, and suppliers as if it's natural.

That's why this is an investment in infrastructure. Each stage makes your organization more capable of executing whatever strategy you throw at it. Skip the belonging work, and you're building a plan on a foundation of chaos.

ROI Trajectory by Maturity Stage

Maturity Stage	Retention ROI	Productivity ROI	Collaboration ROI	Innovation ROI	Operational Impact
Stage 1: Awareness	High replacement costs from variable turnover	Significant productivity loss from disengagement	Project delays from siloed information	Minimal idea implementation	Crisis management mode; reactive leadership
Stage 2: Experimentation	Measurable turnover reduction in pilot areas	Noticeable productivity gains in targeted teams	Improved cross-team project completion	Increased idea generation where practices applied	Localized improvements; proof of concept
Stage 3: Integration	Substantial reduction in regrettable turnover	Clear productivity improvement through standardized practices	Notable reduction in project cycle time	Meaningful improvement in innovation throughput	System-wide capability building
Stage 4: Optimization	Turnover significantly below the industry average	Compound productivity gains from pillar integration	Significant increase in cross-functional collaboration effectiveness	Accelerated innovation cycles	Competitive advantage emergence
Stage 5: Continuous Innovation	Retention stability during market disruption	Maintained productivity during high-change periods	Ecosystem collaboration extends to partners/clients	Self-sustaining innovation culture with high implementation rates	Market leadership through the ability to handle change

Financial Impact Progression

These tables show how business outcomes improve as organizations develop belonging maturity. The frameworks demonstrate how belonging conditions translate into measurable improvements in retention, productivity, collaboration, and innovation.

Chapter 5: How Organizations Actually Improve

Belonging Maturity Stages: Business Impact Across Cost, Revenue, and Capability

Stage	Cost Impact	Revenue Impact	Capability Investment
Stage 1	Baseline: high replacement and inefficiency costs	Missed opportunities from execution gaps	Defensive spending on retention
Stage 2	Measurable cost reductions from pilot area improvements	Limited revenue impact	Experimental investment in belonging practices
Stage 3	Substantial cost savings from retention gains	Revenue acceleration from faster execution	Strategic investment in infrastructure
Stage 4	Compound cost savings from productivity gains	Revenue premium from collaborative advantage	Optimizing investment for scale
Stage 5	Sustained cost savings plus crisis resilience	Revenue premium from innovation leadership	Continuous innovation investment

How Strategic Advantages Evolve

As organizations mature in belonging, they develop stronger capabilities that directly impact how they compete and execute. Instead of tracking employee sentiment, this reveals structural capabilities that alter how work is done.

Change Adaptation shows the most evident progression from reactive chaos to proactive leadership:

- **Stage 1:** Reactive responses; high resistance to change.
- **Stage 2:** Pilot successes that build confidence in change capability.
- **Stage 3:** Systematic change processes that replace ad hoc scrambling.

- **Stage 4:** Rapid adaptation to market shifts through trust infrastructure.
- **Stage 5:** Proactive market leadership; anticipating change before competitors.

Knowledge Transfer evolves from crisis-driven retention to ecosystem collaboration:

- **Stage 1:** Limited transfer; institutional knowledge that is lost when people quit.
- **Stage 2:** Improvement in pilot areas where belonging practices retain key people.
- **Stage 3:** Cross-functional knowledge sharing as silos break down.
- **Stage 4:** Organizational learning systems that capture and spread insights.
- **Stage 5:** Knowledge exchange that extends beyond boundaries to customers, partners, and competitors.

Risk Management shifts from firefighting to resilient infrastructure:

- **Stage 1:** Crisis-driven responses; problems that explode before detection.
- **Stage 2:** Early warning systems that emerge in pilot areas as psychological safety encourages problem identification.
- **Stage 3:** Risk identification processes across the organization.
- **Stage 4:** Predictive analytics that prevent risks before they materialize.

- **Stage 5:** Resilient infrastructure that handles unknown threats and black swan events.

Strategic Execution transforms from implementation gaps to adaptive advantage:

- **Stage 1:** Common execution gaps; strategies that fail in implementation.
- **Stage 2:** Improved execution in pilot areas, demonstrating what's possible.
- **Stage 3:** Consistent strategy deployment across organizational units.
- **Stage 4:** High-velocity execution; strategies implemented faster and more effectively.
- **Stage 5:** Adaptive strategic advantage; ability to execute multiple strategies and pivot quickly.

The pattern is consistent: Each stage builds execution capabilities that enable the next level of competitive performance. Organizations can't skip stages because each level requires the foundational capabilities built in previous stages.

The maturity model turns belonging from wishful thinking into a step-by-step system. Organizations that treat belonging as an infrastructure investment, not a culture program, create measurable advantages that compound over time.

The progression from awareness to continuous innovation changes how leaders approach culture change. Instead of launching broad initiatives and hoping for the best, innovative organizations determine their current position, focus on the next steps, and establish solid foundations before undertaking advanced work.

The ROI shows why belonging maturity is an investment, not an expense. Each stage delivers measurable improvements while building the foundation for the next level. Organizations that advance will upgrade their ability to execute strategy, handle change, and compete in tough markets.

The key factor is that the maturity model provides realistic timelines and advancement requirements that prevent the initiative fatigue plaguing many culture transformation efforts. When leaders understand that the progression from Stage 1 to Stage 2 requires different capabilities than the advancement from Stage 3 to Stage 4, they can allocate resources appropriately and set sustainable expectations.

Trust enables belonging infrastructure, and belonging infrastructure drives business results. But one of the most significant applications gets overlooked: workforce planning. When you understand how belonging changes human performance variables, it transforms how you forecast, budget, and strategize around your most expensive asset—people.

Understanding maturity stages is crucial for planning, but before you can chart a path forward, you need to know where you stand today.

How Organizations Actually Improve

You can't skip stages in belonging development, and trying to do so will waste your time and money. While noble and certainly aspirational, some organizations attempt Stage 4 practices when they're barely at Stage 1, then wonder why nothing sticks. The progression takes eighteen to thirty-six months, when done correctly, with each stage requiring different investments and corresponding payoffs. Early stages prove belonging works in

Chapter 5: How Organizations Actually Improve

your context—you're building credibility with your numbers. Later stages turn that into a competitive advantage in talent wars and execution speed. Your role changes too—Stage 1 involves modeling basic behaviors, while Stage 4 requires competency and predicting cultural risks before they impact performance. Organizations that get this right treat belonging maturity like any other capability: systematic, measured, and built to survive whatever comes next.

But what does this mean for Alicia? Here is how she experiences belonging at each maturity level:

- **Stage 1:** Gets ignored (current story).
- **Stage 2:** Might get heard in pilot teams.
- **Stage 3:** Has processes to capture her input.
- **Stage 4:** Gets proactive support and clear feedback loops.
- **Stage 5:** Becomes the template for onboarding others like her.

Understanding maturity progression helps you plan realistic timelines and resource allocation. But strategic planning assumes accurate baseline data, not wishful thinking about current conditions. The most dangerous assumption in culture work is that leadership perception matches organizational reality.

I've worked with executives who were shocked to discover that their "high-performing culture" was hemorrhaging talent in specific functions, or that their "inclusive environment" was excluding entire demographic groups from decision-making processes. Executive treatment differs dramatically from frontline experience, which means honest assessment becomes the foundation for everything else.

CHAPTER 6

Taking Your Pulse— a Quick Reality Check

The following is the most dangerous phrase I hear from executives: "We already have a great culture here."

Maybe they do. But in my experience, leaders often have a rosier view of belonging conditions than the people experiencing them. Senior executives receive different treatment from frontline employees, so belonging problems often remain hidden from leadership until they escalate into crises.[178]

Executives often have a rosier-than-accurate view of reality. That's why I built this quick diagnostic. This diagnostic helps you determine if belonging is healthy or needs attention, much like checking your organization's vital signs.

First, let's establish your baseline.

---

178 R. G. Netemeyer, J. G. Maxham, and D. R. Lichtenstein, "Store Manager Behaviors and Frontline Employee Performance," *Journal of Marketing Research* 40, no. 3 (2003): 271–286, https://doi.org/10.1509/jmkr.40.3.271.19236.

How This Works

Hagerty and Patusky[179] developed the first psychometrically sound belonging scale, establishing reliability standards and factor structures that inform contemporary organizational applications. Think of it as taking your organization's temperature—it won't diagnose complex conditions, but it'll tell you if something needs attention.

Score each statement from 1 to 5: Rate each statement from 1 (Strongly Disagree) to 5 (Strongly Agree) based on your honest assessment of conditions across your organization, not just your immediate team or the executive level.

To get accurate results, don't score based on your intentions. Score based on what you actually see happening. This reflects established principles in organizational psychology. A meta-analysis of 263 studies reveals that multiple measures are necessary to accurately predict performance.[180]

Don't give yourself credit for initiatives you've launched but haven't yet embedded. Don't average the best and worst units—focus on what's typical.

The Reality Check: Pillar Indicators

Psychological Safety

1 People can share concerns, mistakes, or ideas without fear of negative consequences.

---

179 B. M. Hagerty and K. Patusky, "Developing a Measure of Sense of Belonging," *Nursing Research* 44, no. 1 (1995): 9–13, https://doi.org/10.1097/00006199-199501000-00003.

180 M. S. Christian, A. S. Garza, and J. E. Slaughter, "Work Engagement: A Quantitative Review and Test of Its Relations with Task and Contextual Performance," *Personnel Psychology* 64, no. 1 (2011): 89–136, https://doi.org/10.1111/j.1744-6570.2010.01203.x.

Chapter 6: Taking Your Pulse—a Quick Reality Check

2 The organization enables leaders to admit mistakes and invite candid input from all levels.
3 Disagreements can be raised and addressed constructively.
4 People can question decisions respectfully without backlash.
5 Feedback is given and received with the intent to improve, not punish.

Inclusion

1 Diverse perspectives are actively sought and factored into decisions.
2 Leaders distribute recognition equitably across different groups and roles.
3 Leaders ensure meetings and processes allow every voice to be heard.
4 People with differing viewpoints are treated with respect and curiosity.
5 Policies and practices address the needs of a diverse workforce.

Support

1 People have timely access to the tools, resources, and training they need to succeed.
2 Managers regularly check in on workload and help remove barriers.
3 Guidance and mentoring are available when needed.
4 Requests for help are met with responsiveness and respect.

5 Leaders advocate for their teams when resources or support are needed.

Connection

1 People have trusted colleagues they can turn to for advice or help.
2 Teams collaborate and share information across departments.
3 Leaders invest time in relationship building beyond daily tasks.
4 Celebrations or recognition events foster a sense of togetherness.
5 Informal connections happen naturally, even across role levels or geographies.

Purpose

1 People understand how their work contributes to organizational goals.
2 Individual contributions are recognized in ways that connect to the mission.
3 Decisions made by leaders reflect an understanding of the value of different roles.
4 Organizational priorities are communicated clearly and consistently.
5 People believe their work makes a meaningful difference to customers, colleagues, or the community.

Chapter 6: Taking Your Pulse—a Quick Reality Check

Self-Check Mini-Audit— Audit Scorecard Table (for filling in)

Pillar	Item #	Statement	Score (1–5)
Psychological Safety	1	I can share concerns, mistakes, or ideas without fear of negative consequences.	[ ]
	2	Leaders admit mistakes and invite candid input.	[ ]
	3	Disagreements can be raised constructively.	[ ]
	4	People can question decisions respectfully without backlash.	[ ]
	5	Feedback is given/received with the intention of improving, not punishing.	[ ]
Inclusion	6	Diverse perspectives are actively sought and factored into decisions.	[ ]
	7	Leaders distribute recognition equitably across different groups and roles.	[ ]
	8	Leaders ensure meetings and processes allow every voice to be heard.	[ ]
	9	People with differing viewpoints are treated with respect and curiosity.	[ ]
	10	Policies and practices address the needs of a diverse workforce.	[ ]
Support	11	People have timely access to the tools, resources, and training they need to succeed.	[ ]
	12	Managers regularly check in on workload and help remove barriers.	[ ]
	13	Guidance and mentoring are available when needed.	[ ]
	14	Requests for help are met with responsiveness and respect.	[ ]
	15	Leaders advocate for their teams when resources or support are needed.	[ ]

Connection	16	People have trusted colleagues they can turn to for advice or help.	[ ]
	17	Teams collaborate and share information across departments.	[ ]
	18	Leaders invest time in relationship building beyond daily tasks.	[ ]
	19	Celebrations or recognition events foster a sense of togetherness.	[ ]
	20	Informal connections happen naturally, even across role levels or geographies.	[ ]
Purpose	21	People understand how their work contributes to organizational goals.	[ ]
	22	Individual contributions are recognized in ways that connect to the mission.	[ ]
	23	Decisions made by leaders reflect an understanding of the value of different roles.	[ ]
	24	Organizational priorities are communicated clearly and consistently.	[ ]
	25	People believe their work makes a meaningful difference to customers, colleagues, or the community.	[ ]

Scoring and Interpretation

Per Pillar Score Ranges (max 25 points each)

- **21–25:** Strong—pillar conditions are robust; sustain through reinforcement.
- **15–20:** Moderate—pillar conditions are inconsistent; targeted improvement will yield gains.
- **Below 15:** Weak—pillar conditions are underdeveloped; high-ROI opportunity area.

Chapter 6: Taking Your Pulse—a Quick Reality Check

Composite Score (max 125 points total)

- 105–125: High Belonging—likely in Stage 4 or 5 of the maturity model.
- 85–104: Moderate Belonging—likely in Stage 2 or 3; targeted actions can accelerate progress.
- **Below 85:** Low Belonging—likely in Stage 1 or early Stage 2; foundational action required across multiple pillars.

This mini-audit gives you directional insight, but improvement requires a comprehensive diagnosis.

What the Patterns Tell You

The most revealing part of this audit is the variance between pillars. Rarely, organizations will see uniformly strong or weak across all five areas.

More commonly, I see patterns like high Psychological Safety and Purpose scores but low Support and Connection scores. Or strong Inclusion and Support with weak Safety and Purpose. These patterns reveal specific problems.

For example, organizations with high Purpose but low Safety often have inspiring missions but cultures where people are afraid to articulate known problems. Organizations with high Support but low Inclusion tend to be helpful but homogeneous—they take care of people who fit the existing mold.

The organizations that struggle most are those with high variance between pillars. When some belonging conditions are strong while others are weak, it creates cognitive dissonance. When people receive mixed signals about belonging, they tend to default to the most negative interpretation. Mixed signals about belonging often confuse people more than consistently poor conditions.[181]

People get mixed signals about whether they truly belong.

What This Doesn't Tell You

This mini-audit has intentional limitations. It doesn't break down results by different groups or show how belonging affects business outcomes. It doesn't provide implementation road maps or specific intervention priorities. The mini-audit is designed to provide you with enough information to determine whether a more comprehensive diagnosis is warranted.

The mini-audit also reflects your perspective, not that of your workforce. If you scored high but haven't actually asked your employees about their sense of belonging, there's likely a gap between your perception and their reality.

Studies on leadership perception gaps confirm this pattern—executives consistently overestimate the culture conditions compared to those of frontline employees.[182] The higher you sit in the organization, the rosier things look.

Using Your Results

If your composite score surprised you—either higher or lower than expected—that's valuable information. It suggests that belonging conditions may differ from what leadership visibility implies.

---

181 L. Festinger, *A Theory of Cognitive Dissonance* (Stanford University Press, 1957).
182 Netemeyer et al., 2003.

Chapter 6: Taking Your Pulse—a Quick Reality Check

If specific pillars scored significantly lower than others, those are your highest-leverage improvement opportunities. Focus on your weakest areas first. The minor improvements will have a big impact.

If your scores were consistently moderate across all pillars, you likely have an opportunity for improvement. Organizations that enhance their belonging infrastructure often experience compounding benefits across metrics, including retention, performance, and innovation.[183]

The Next Step Decision

Based on patterns, here's how I'd interpret your results for next steps:

1. Above 105, you're likely already benefiting from belonging as a unique advantage. The question is whether you're measuring and protecting those conditions, especially during periods of change or growth.
2. Scored 85–104? You have a moderate level of belonging with significant upside potential. The ROI case for improvement of belonging is strong, and you likely have pockets of excellence to learn from internally.
3. Scoring below 85 indicates that foundational work is needed, but also presents a significant opportunity for improvement.

---

[183] BetterUp, 2019, 2024.

Why This Matters Right Now

Organizations that thrive during uncertainty are those with a strong sense of belonging infrastructure in place before the uncertainty arises. When trust, inclusion, support, connection, and purpose are already embedded in how work gets done, teams adapt faster and recover more quickly from disruption.

Crisis resilience research supports this—organizations with strong social infrastructure maintain their performance under stress, while those without it experience rapid capability degradation.[184] You can't build a sense of belonging when you need it most.

The organizations that struggle are those that attempt to foster a sense of belonging during a crisis. By then, people are already in protective mode, making the trust-building work much harder.

This mini-audit provides directional insight, but putting real structure behind it requires comprehensive baseline measurement. Organizations that act on surface-level assessment often misallocate resources or attempt interventions their culture isn't ready to support.

Assessment reveals where you are. Implementation determines where you go. The gap between recognizing your belonging gaps and closing them is where most initiatives fail—not from a lack of commitment, but from a lack of execution.

---

184 Sutcliffe & Vogus, 2003.

CHAPTER 7

Implementation—Getting Started Monday Morning

The following is the question I get most often after explaining the Belonging Standard and the Belonging Maturity Model: "Okay, Eric, this makes sense conceptually. But how does this get implemented?"

That's the right question. Frameworks mean nothing without implementation. Implementation fails without design, proper sequencing, and continuous reinforcement.

This chapter shows you how to implement belonging in your organization.

Why Most Implementation Fails

Prosci's 2024 research on change resistance shows that 67 percent of employees become skeptical of new initiatives when previous efforts lacked follow-through, creating what researchers term "change fatigue syndrome."[185] The failure pattern is predictable across organizations, though it manifests differently in each context. What's frustrating is that these failures are avoidable, they stem from treating belonging as a program instead of infrastructure.

Learning from Failures

Beyond the common implementation pitfalls, peer-reviewed research identifies three structural factors that cause belonging initiatives to fail even when well resourced and leadership supported:

- **Institutional Structure Conflicts:** When belonging practices conflict with existing institutional structures—hierarchical decision-making, competitive performance systems, or resource allocation processes—employees experience cognitive dissonance that undermines trust in the initiative.
- **Insufficient Procedural Integration:** Isolated psychological tactics (team building, awareness training, culture surveys) are insufficient without embedding belonging into operational procedures. This explains why Stage 3 integration work is nonnegotiable for sustainable results.
- **Cultural Misalignment:** What works in one organizational context may have limited or counterproductive effects in another, requiring careful adaptation rather

---

185 Prosci, *Global Insights about Organizational Change Today: Change Fatigue and Resistance* (2024), https://www.prosci.com/blog/global-insights-about-organizational-change-today.

than wholesale adoption of belonging practices from different environments.

Here are some examples of how belonging initiatives are likely to derail.

The Training-Only Approach

Leadership launches belonging workshops for all managers, investing significant budget in facilitators and materials, but doesn't change performance evaluation criteria or meeting structures.

Managers attend sessions, nod enthusiastically, complete the feedback forms positively, then revert to old behaviors when quarterly pressure hits. They run the same meetings, make decisions the same way, and handle conflicts using familiar patterns.

Six months later, employee feedback reveals nothing has changed in daily operations. People report that their managers "talk about belonging" but still interrupt them in meetings or dismiss their ideas without discussion.

The Pilot Trap

A few high-performing teams implement belonging practices successfully, generating positive metrics and enthusiastic testimonials that leadership showcases in company meetings. These teams often have naturally collaborative managers who were already creating inclusive environments.

Leadership declares victory and attempts to scale the approach organization-wide without manager enablement or process integration. Most teams struggle to replicate the pilot results because they lack the underlying skills, time allocation, or cultural context that made the pilots successful.

This leads to inconsistent implementation and employee cynicism about leadership commitment, with people saying things like the following: "It worked for Sarah's team, but our manager doesn't really get it."

The Survey-Response Cycle

Annual engagement surveys reveal belonging issues through low scores on questions about psychological safety or inclusion, prompting HR to launch initiatives like "inclusion councils" or "psychological safety training."

These programs run for six to twelve months with dedicated project managers and budget, complete with logos, communication campaigns, and regular updates in company newsletters. When survey results show minimal improvement—often because the underlying systems and processes haven't changed—leadership questions the ROI and quietly reduces resources.

The inclusion council stops meeting regularly, training sessions get postponed, and employees feel their input was ignored. This creates deeper cynicism for the next culture initiative.

The Champion Dependency

A passionate CHRO or executive champions belonging, driving impressive improvements through personal attention and resource allocation. They attend team meetings, check in with managers personally, and ensure belonging stays on the agenda in leadership discussions. This creates real momentum and measurable results.

When that champion leaves or shifts focus to other

priorities—perhaps a merger, budget crisis, or new strategic initiative—belonging practices gradually fade because they weren't embedded in systems and processes. They were dependent on individual advocacy rather than organizational infrastructure. New priorities take over, and belonging work gets deprioritized as "nice to have" rather than business critical.

The Competing Priorities Problem

Even when belonging initiatives launch successfully, they often compete for attention with operational demands. When sales targets are missed, customer complaints spike, or product launches get delayed, managers naturally focus on immediate business problems.

Belonging practices—holding inclusive meetings, checking in on team members, providing development feedback—get postponed until "things calm down." But things never calm down in most organizations, so belonging work gets continuously deferred.

Leaders have plenty of commitment. They genuinely believe belonging matters and want their organizations to be places where people thrive. They just treat belonging as an add-on rather than essential infrastructure.

When belonging competes with "real work" for attention, real work wins every time operational pressures increase.[186] This is because they haven't structured belonging as part of how real work gets done.

Add-on programs fail because they compete with core work instead of becoming part of it.[187] Belonging either gets embedded

---

186 Deloitte, 2025; BetterUp, 2019.
187 D. L. Fixsen, S. F. Naoom, K. A. Blase, R. M. Friedman, and F. Wallace, Implementation Research: A Synthesis of the Literature (University of South Florida, 2005).

in how work gets done or it gets abandoned when things get tough.

The test is whether belonging practices survive when deadlines are tight, budgets are strained, and everyone is working longer hours.

To Make Belonging Stick— Three Changes Must Occur

1 **Integration over addition:** Build belonging into existing processes instead of creating separate programs.[188] This means redesigning how meetings run, how decisions get made, and how performance gets evaluated, rather than adding belonging training on top of existing workflows.
2 **System design over individual behavior:** Change how work gets done instead of hoping people will just "be nicer."[189] Focus on creating structures that make inclusive behavior easier and more natural, rather than relying on individual motivation and good intentions.
3 **Continuous measurement over periodic campaigns:** Measure belonging continuously, not just during annual culture surveys.[190] This means tracking belonging conditions monthly or quarterly, the same way you track revenue or customer satisfaction, so you can spot problems and course-correct before they become crises.

---

188 A. Miranda-Wolff, *Cultures of Belonging: Building Inclusive Organizations That Last* (HarperCollins Leadership, 2022).
189 Edmondson & Lei, 2014.
190 i4cp, 2024.

Chapter 7: Implementation—Getting Started Monday Morning

Make these changes, and belonging becomes part of how work gets done.[191] Skip these changes, and belonging becomes another well-intentioned initiative that fades when attention shifts elsewhere.

The Voice of the Employee Method: Systematic Problem-Solving

The most effective approach I've witnessed gets employees directly involved in identifying problems and creating solutions. This Voice of the Employee method works because it tackles the real issue behind most culture problems: People don't believe leadership will actually act on their feedback.

The process has four phases:

1 **Phase 1: Safe Venting (Day 1):** Give employees structured time to air frustrations without leadership in the room. One participant told me: "We spent the first thirty minutes talking about how this was a safe space, and I think that context really opened up the group to share the most important feedback." The goal is problem identification, not just complaining.

2 **Phase 2: Future Visioning (Day 2):** Move from problems to solutions. What would this organization look like at its best? What conditions do people need to thrive? This Appreciative Inquiry approach gets people energized and invested in change.

3 **Phase 3: Rollout (Weeks 3–8):** Take the process to 15 percent of employees through voluntary focus groups. Run three-hour sessions where people can speak openly

---

191 BetterUp, 2024; Deloitte, 2025.

about belonging conditions and help create improvement recommendations.

4 **Phase 4: Leadership Action (Ongoing):** Leadership gets all feedback—including direct quotes—and commits to tackling the top three to five systemic recommendations with monthly progress updates.

This approach hits all five belonging pillars: psychological safety through careful process design, inclusion through input collection, support through leadership's commitment to act, connection through collaborative problem-solving, and purpose by linking individual input to organizational change.

The payoff: belonging infrastructure that employees own, not something executives impose from above.

The method works, but only when you build it on solid foundations. At that start-up, we could implement Voice of the Employee successfully because we understood our baseline conditions and had executive commitment to act on what we learned. Without that foundation, even the best employee feedback process becomes another initiative that raises expectations and delivers disappointment.

That's why belonging work starts with knowing exactly where you stand.

The Implementation Sequence That Works

Successful implementation of belonging follows a predictable sequence across organizations. These steps happen in order; however, you can move through them faster with the right approach.

Chapter 7: Implementation—Getting Started Monday Morning

Phase 1: Foundation (Days 1–30)
The first month determines whether your belonging effort will have staying power or become another failed culture initiative. The critical work starts with executives.

- **Executive alignment comes first.** Kotter's research on change management confirms this: Without sustained executive commitment, transformation efforts fail, regardless of initial enthusiasm.[192] Most leaders already agree on the importance of belonging. The challenge is achieving shared commitment to measurement, accountability, and implementation across multiple quarters.[193]
    - Will belonging metrics be reviewed alongside financial metrics in quarterly business reviews?
    - Will pillar improvements be included in executive performance objectives?
    - Will resources be maintained for the infrastructure supporting belonging, even when operational pressures increase?
- **Baseline measurement** establishes where you are rather than where you think you are. The full audit provides validated data across all five pillars, segmented by role level, department, and other relevant dimensions. This serves as the foundation for your improvement planning.[194]
- **Target identification** focuses effort on the highest-ROI opportunities. Rather than trying to improve everything simultaneously, identify one or two pillar areas where

---
192 Kotter, 1996.
193 Deloitte, 2025.
194 BetterUp, 2024.

improvement will have the most significant business impact based on your baseline data and organizational priorities.[195]

The test is whether they manage it like revenue.
If Alicia is your litmus test, consider the following:

- **Phase 1:** Executive alignment means asking, "Would our executives know if we had an Alicia problem?"
- **Phase 2:** "Does manager enablement prepare managers to catch Alicia's contributions before they get lost?"
- **Phase 3:** "Does process embedding mean Alicia's experience becomes impossible, not just unlikely?"

Phase 2: Enablement (Days 31–60)

Month two focuses on building the capabilities required to execute belonging practices consistently. This is where good intentions meet operational reality.

Middle managers make or break belonging initiatives. Belonging doesn't scale through executive vision or employee enthusiasm; it scales through manager behavior. If managers don't change their daily behavior, nothing happens.[196] Remember Alicia's manager? That's where belonging lives or dies.

Manager training covers the basics: running meetings where everyone gets heard, checking on workload before people burn out, building genuine relationships beyond task assignments, and helping people see how their work matters to the bigger picture.

---

195 Edmondson & Lei, 2014; Deloitte, 2025.
196 K. J. Klein and J. S. Sorra, "The Challenge of Innovation Implementation," *Academy of Management Review* 21, no. 4 (1996): 1055–1080, https://doi.org/10.5465/amr.1996.9704071863.

Chapter 7: Implementation—Getting Started Monday Morning

Belonging scores should be reported alongside revenue and margin data. If you bury belonging metrics in separate HR dashboards, then you've just told everyone it's not an absolute business priority.

Target the specific gaps your audit revealed. Pick one of two pillars that scored lowest and design interventions that will show visible improvement within sixty days.

Phase 3: Integration (Days 61–90)

The third month determines whether belonging practices become sustainable infrastructure or fade as attention shifts to other priorities.

Pilot expansion takes successful practices from Phase 2 and scales them to additional teams or departments. The key is maintaining quality and measurement discipline as the scope increases.

Mid-cycle measurement captures whether your initial interventions are producing intended outcomes. This data informs adjustments and provides proof points for continued investment.

Build belonging into your existing processes: hiring practices, performance reviews, promotion criteria, strategic planning processes, and change management protocols.

Scale planning prepares for organization-wide implementation based on what you've learned from the first ninety days. This includes resource requirements, timeline expectations, and governance structures for sustained implementation.

Road Maps by Maturity Stage

What you do first depends entirely on your level of maturity. Stage 1 organizations need different interventions than Stage 3 organizations.

Stage 1 → Stage 2 Road Map
Priority:

- Building measurement discipline and pilot proof points

Key actions:

- Adopt the Belonging Standard.
- Conduct baseline audit.
- Launch targeted pilots in key departments.
- Establish executive sponsorship and governance.

Success metrics:

- Shared belonging language.
- Baseline pillar scores.
- Two or three successful pilot cases with measurable improvement.

Illustration:

- A Stage 1 technology company conducted its first belonging audit and discovered Psychological Safety scored 11/25 while Purpose scored 22/25. They launched targeted safety interventions in engineering teams, including structured retrospectives and manager vulnerability training. Four months later, Safety scores rose to 18/25, and voluntary turnover in engineering dropped by 6 percent.

Implementation Road Map (Stage 1 → 2):

- **Phase 1: Foundation (Days 1–30):** Adopt Belonging Standard, conduct baseline audit, secure executive sponsorship.
- **Phase 2: Pilot Selection (Days 31–60):** Identify high-impact units, design targeted interventions, and establish measurement cadence.
- **Phase 3: Early Implementation (Days 61–90):** Launch pilots, track pillar movement, document learnings for scale.

Stage 2 → Stage 3 Road Map
Priority:

- Expanding measurement frequency and embedding manager accountability.

Key actions:

- Increase measurement to quarterly cycles.
- Embed belonging metrics in quarterly business reviews.
- Implement role-specific enablement for managers.
- Connect pilot results to business outcomes.

Success metrics:

- Quarterly belonging data.
- Manager competency development.
- Belonging considerations in formal processes.

Illustration:

- A Stage 2 organization with Inclusion gains but persistent Support friction applied a targeted intervention: manager retraining in capacity scoping and debrief consistency. Six months later, team-level retention improved by 9 percent, and Support sentiment rose by twelve points.

Implementation Road Map (Stage 2 → 3):

- **Phase 1: Foundation (Days 1–30):** Align the executive team; identify target pillars and pilot units.
- **Phase 2: Enablement (Days 31–60):** Train managers on weak pillars, embed belonging metrics into routine ops.
- **Phase 3: Integration (Days 61–90):** Expand pilots, capture mid-cycle data, finalize scale plan.

Later-stage road maps activate additional layers: people analytics, system telemetry, and auto-generated nudges for next-best actions. These features increase intervention speed and reduce the lag time for escalation.

Stage 3 → Stage 4 Road Map
Priority:

- Achieving consistency and predictive capability.

Key actions:

- Align belonging performance with leader incentives.
- Implement predictive analytics for risk identification.
- Benchmark against external organizations.
- Integrate belonging into strategic change management—success metrics.

Encompass consistent belonging scores across units, predictive risk identification, and belonging-informed strategic decisions.

Illustration:

- A Stage 3 financial services firm embedded consideration of belonging into its acquisition strategy. Before acquiring a fintech start-up, they assessed cultural compatibility using pillar scores. Post-merger integration preserved high-belonging conditions in both organizations, resulting in 89 percent talent retention versus the industry average of 72 percent during acquisitions.

Implementation Road Map (Stage 3 → 4):

- **Phase 1: Analytics Development (Days 1–30):** Implement

predictive belonging analytics, establish risk threshold alerts, and create executive dashboards.
- **Phase 2: Strategic Integration (Days 31–60):** Embed belonging impact assessments in major decisions, align leader incentives with belonging outcomes.
- **Phase 3: Optimization (Days 61–90):** Activate predictive interventions, benchmark against top performers, and refine governance structures.

Stage 4 → Stage 5 Road Map
Priority:

- Continuous innovation and competitive differentiation.

Key actions:

- Refresh belonging framework with new research.
- Establish external thought leadership.
- Use belonging for talent attraction and brand differentiation.
- Contribute to industry-best practices.

Success metrics:

- Sustained high performance.
- External recognition.
- Influence on industry standards.

Illustration:

Chapter 7: Implementation—Getting Started Monday Morning

- A Stage 4 healthcare organization became an industry case study by publishing its correlation data on patient safety. Their innovation in measuring Connection density across care teams influenced Joint Commission standards and attracted top clinical talent seeking evidence-based culture practices.

Implementation Road Map (Stage 4 → 5):

- **Phase 1: Innovation Lab (Days 1–30):** Refresh Belonging Standard with the latest research, pilot next-generation measurement tools, and establish external partnerships.
- **Phase 2: Thought Leadership (Days 31–60):** Share best practices externally, contribute to industry standards, position belonging as a competitive differentiator.
- **Phase 3: Continuous Evolution (Days 61–90):** Implement adaptive belonging infrastructure, establish an innovation pipeline, and sustain the market leadership position.

Advanced Features by Stage:

- Later-stage road maps activate additional layers: people analytics, system telemetry, and auto-generated nudges for next-best actions. These features increase intervention speed and reduce the lag time for escalation.

Stage Advancement Requirements

From Stage	To Stage	Required Evidence	Typical Timeline	Critical Success Factors
1 → 2	Awareness → Experimentation	Baseline audit completed, executive alignment, pilot selection	3–6 months	Shared belonging language, measurement discipline
2 → 3	Experimentation → Integration	Pilot ROI demonstrated, manager enablement, process updates	6–12 months	Manager accountability, business case validation
3 → 4	Integration → Optimization	Consistent scores across units, predictive analytics, and strategic integration	12–18 months	Executive governance, belonging-informed decisions
4 → 5	Optimization → Continuous Innovation	Sustained high performance, external recognition, and industry influence	18+ months	Innovation in practices, external thought leadership

Progression Indicators by Stage

- **Stage 1:** Ad hoc belonging discussions → formal framework adoption
- **Stage 2:** Isolated pilots → coordinated experimentation with measurement
- **Stage 3:** Program-based → process-embedded belonging practices
- **Stage 4:** Reactive management → predictive belonging analytics

Chapter 7: Implementation—Getting Started Monday Morning

- **Stage 5:** Internal focus → external influence and continuous innovation

Note: Organizations can accelerate progression but cannot skip stages. Each stage builds foundational capabilities required for the next level of maturity.

On a more granular level the first month's weekly objectives are as follows:

First Month Implementation Timeline

Cross-Pillar Sequencing Logic

Most organizations discover that their pillar scores are uneven—high in some areas, low in others. This creates sequencing decisions about which pillars to address first.

Here's the order that works:

- **Address Psychological Safety first** if it's actively eroding retention or performance. Without safety, other pillar improvements are fragile because people remain in protective mode.[197]
- **Build Connection** before scaling cross-functional initiatives. Collaboration fails without underlying trust and relationship infrastructure.[198]
- **Strengthen Purpose** during large-scale change to stabilize engagement when other organizational elements are shifting.[199]

---

197 Edmondson, 1999; Edmondson & Lei, 2014.
198 Harter et al., 2020.
199 Pratt & Ashforth, 2003.

- **Address Support gaps** in high-demand functions to prevent burnout and maintain performance under pressure.[200]
- **Improve Inclusion** once safety and connection provide the foundation for productive disagreement and diverse input.[201]

The key insight is that pillar improvements amplify each other when sequenced properly but can conflict when implemented simultaneously without consideration of interdependencies.[202] Change management research supports this—trying to implement multiple interventions simultaneously creates interference rather than acceleration.[203] Sequence matters more than speed.

Cultural Implementation Considerations

Implementation timelines and tactics must be adapted for cultural context:

- **Relationship-First Cultures:** Connection building may need to precede other pillar development.
- **Hierarchy-Respectful Cultures:** Safety building requires different approaches that work within existing authority structures.
- **Consensus-Building Cultures:** Inclusion practices may take longer but create stronger buy-in once established.

---

200 Bakker & Demerouti, 2007.
201 Edmondson & Lei, 2014.
202 Edmondson & Lei, 2014; Harter et al., 2020.
203 A. A. Armenakis and A. G. Bedeian, "Organizational Change: A Review of Theory and Research in the 1990s," *Journal of Management* 25, no. 3 (1999): 293–315, https://doi.org/10.1177/014920639902500303.

- **Achievement-Oriented Cultures:** Purpose alignment and measurement discipline may accelerate adoption.

Use the same foundational framework but adapt your implementation approach to work with, rather than against, existing cultural strengths.

Who Does What: The Leadership Reality

Belonging doesn't scale by accident. It scales when leaders at every level consistently demonstrate specific behaviors, apply the Belonging Standard in decisions, and stay accountable for measurable outcomes.

Most belonging initiatives fail because they assume good intentions translate into consistent action. They don't. You need explicit role accountability mapped to maturity stages so leaders know precisely what's expected of them and how their actions advance the organization's belonging capability.

How Responsibilities Evolve by Stage

Belonging responsibilities aren't static—they evolve as the organization moves through maturity stages. What executives need to do at Stage 1 is different from what they need to do at Stage 4, and the same applies to managers and employees.

Stage 1–2: Awareness to Experimentation

At early stages, the work focuses on building a foundation and proving the concept.

Executives

Executives need to publicly commit to the Belonging Standard, authorize the baseline audit, and sponsor visible pilot projects. This is about resource allocation and organizational signal-sending.

Behaviors include the following:

- Allocating dedicated budget for belonging measurement.
- Attending pilot team meetings personally.
- Asking "How does this decision affect belonging?" in strategy discussions.
- Sharing their own mistakes openly in leadership communications to model psychological safety.

Managers

Managers begin applying pillar principles in team meetings, feedback processes, and recognition practices. They're learning the behaviors while modeling them for their teams.

Behaviors include the following:

- Starting meetings by asking "What am I missing?" to encourage diverse input.
- Checking in with quiet team members privately after meetings.
- Acknowledging their own uncertainty when making decisions.
- Giving recognition that specifically connects individual contributions to team impact.

Employees

Employees participate in pilots, provide candid feedback, and engage in early voice forums. Their role is to test whether belonging practices are effective and provide honest feedback about what works.

Behaviors include the following:

- Volunteering for pilot programs despite initial skepticism.
- Sharing honest concerns in feedback sessions even when uncomfortable.
- Offering suggestions for process improvements.
- Supporting new hires during onboarding without being asked.

Stage 3: Integration

At this stage, belonging transitions from an experimental practice to an operational one.

Executives

Executives embed belonging metrics into business scorecards, tie pillar targets to leader incentives, and ensure resource allocation aligns with audit priorities. Belonging becomes an integral part of how business performance is measured and managed.

Behaviors include the following:

- Reviewing belonging scores in the same meetings where they discuss revenue.
- Making belonging competency a requirement for leadership promotion.
- Using belonging data when deciding on reorganizations or budget cuts.
- Modeling inclusive decision-making by explicitly

seeking input from underrepresented voices before major announcements.

Managers

Managers use team-level pillar reports to guide development plans and model inclusion, safety, and connection in daily routines. They transition from learning about belonging practices to consistently executing them.

Behaviors include the following:

- Starting each week by reviewing their team's pillar scores and planning specific actions to address weak areas.
- Proactively checking on workload and barriers rather than waiting for people to ask for help.
- Facilitating team discussions where everyone speaks before decisions are made.
- Celebrating mistakes that lead to learning while addressing performance issues directly.

Employees

Employees actively engage in cross-team initiatives and take responsibility for providing peer support and sharing knowledge. They become belonging practitioners, not just beneficiaries.

Behaviors include the following:

- Voluntarily joining cross-functional projects to build connections.
- Mentoring colleagues from different departments.
- Speaking up when they see exclusionary behavior in meetings.

- Sharing knowledge freely instead of hoarding information for job security.

Stage 4–5: Optimization to Continuous Innovation

At advanced stages, belonging becomes a strategic capability and competitive advantage.

Executives

Executives utilize belonging data in strategic decisions, such as market expansions, mergers and acquisitions (M&A), and reorganizations. They represent progress in belonging, as seen in investor and brand communications, which is part of their external positioning.

Behaviors include the following:

- Conducting belonging assessments during acquisition due diligence.
- Using belonging metrics to predict which teams can handle increased responsibility during expansion.
- Sharing belonging case studies in board presentations and investor meetings.
- Personally recruiting talent by highlighting the organization's belonging infrastructure rather than just compensation packages.

Managers

Managers sustain high pillar scores through continuous enablement, anticipate belonging risks during change, and maintain feedback loops that prevent regression.

Behaviors include the following:

- Identifying early warning signs of belonging breakdown (like increased sick days or reduced meeting participation).
- Adapting their management approach when team composition changes.
- Seeking feedback on their own belonging leadership from peers and direct reports.
- Sharing their belonging practices with other managers across the organization.

Employees

Employees cocreate improvements, mentor peers on belonging practices, and contribute to innovation in belonging enablement. They become belonging leaders regardless of formal title.

Behaviors include the following:

- Proposing new ways to improve team belonging based on their daily experience.
- Coaching colleagues on how to navigate difficult conversations safely.
- Taking initiative to connect isolated team members with broader networks.
- Volunteering to facilitate belonging workshops for other teams.

Common Accountability Pitfalls and Fixes

Pitfall: Executive Lip Service

- *What it looks like:* Executives talk about belonging in

all-hands meetings but don't change their own behavior. They interrupt people, make decisions without input, or dismiss concerns as "not strategic."
- *Fix:* Implement 360-degree feedback specifically on belonging behaviors. Tie executive bonuses to team belonging scores. Require executives to share one personal mistake or learning in each quarterly business review.

Pitfall: Manager Role Confusion

- *What it looks like:* Managers think belonging means being "nice" or avoiding difficult conversations. They stop giving direct feedback, avoid addressing performance issues, or treat belonging as separate from business results.
- *Fix:* Provide specific behavioral scripts for difficult conversations that maintain psychological safety. Train managers to separate person from performance in feedback. Show managers how belonging practices improve rather than compromise business outcomes.

Pitfall: Employee Passive Participation

- *What it looks like:* Employees participate in belonging surveys and training but don't change their own behavior toward colleagues. They expect managers to create belonging without taking personal responsibility.
- *Fix:* Create peer feedback mechanisms where employees give input on one another's belonging behaviors. Include

belonging contributions in performance reviews. Recognize employees who actively support colleagues rather than just those who receive support.

Pitfall: Stage Mismatched Expectations

- *What it looks like:* Organizations expect Stage 1 employees to behave like Stage 4 practitioners, leading to frustration and cynicism. Or Stage 4 organizations revert to Stage 2 practices during pressure.
- *Fix:* Clearly communicate stage-appropriate expectations. Provide different development paths for different maturity levels. Protect advanced practices during organizational stress rather than reverting to easier approaches.

Pitfall: Accountability Without Support

- *What it looks like:* Leaders are held accountable for belonging outcomes but aren't given the skills, time, or resources to succeed. This creates defensive behavior and gaming of metrics.
- *Fix:* Pair accountability with skill development. Provide coaching for leaders struggling with belonging practices. Ensure resource allocation supports belonging expectations rather than competing with them.

Chapter 7: Implementation—Getting Started Monday Morning

Role Accountability by Maturity Stage

Maturity Stage	Executives	Managers	Employees
Stage 1: Awareness	Publicly commit to the Belonging Standard. Approve baseline Audit—sponsor visible pilot efforts.	Model basic belonging behaviors in team meetings. Gather informal feedback on pillar conditions.	Participate in pilots. Share candid feedback through initial forums or surveys.
Stage 2: Experimentation	Link early audit results to business priorities. Fund targeted pilot initiatives in priority units.	Apply pillar-specific practices in pilots. Track early improvements. Share learnings with peers.	Engage in pilot programs. Offer suggestions to improve team-level conditions for belonging.
Stage 3: Integration	Embed belonging KPIs into business scorecards. Tie leader incentives to pillar improvement targets.	Use team-level pillar reports for development plans. Ensure daily routines support prioritized pillars.	Participate in cross-team projects. Take responsibility for peer support and inclusion behaviors.
Stage 4: Optimization	Use belonging metrics in strategic decision-making (M&A, reorganizations, market expansions). Benchmark against high-performing peers.	Maintain high pillar scores through continuous enablement and support. Anticipate belonging risks during change.	Cocreate improvements. Mentor peers on belonging practices. Contribute to innovation efforts.
Stage 5: Continuous Innovation	Refresh the Belonging Standard with new research—position belonging as a differentiator in brand and talent strategy.	Sustain gains by evolving practices. Share innovations across the organization.	Lead by example in adopting new belonging practices. Actively participate in culture innovation cycles.

The Behavioral Chain That Makes It Work

What I've observed across successful belonging transformations is a specific behavioral chain that underpins maturity movement:

- *Executive modeling:* Leaders set the tone by demonstrating vulnerability, inclusive decision-making, and visible recognition of others. When executives model belonging behaviors, it gives managers permission and employees confidence to do the same.

- *Manager application:* Managers translate executive signals into daily routines: inclusive meetings, proactive support, and connection-building rituals. This is where belonging either becomes a reality or remains an aspiration.

- *Employee participation:* Employees respond by engaging more fully, offering ideas, and supporting peers. When they see consistent signals from executives and managers, they shift from protective behavior to contributive behavior.

- *Reinforcement and measurement:* Behaviors are reinforced through recognition, promotion criteria, and regular measurement. What gets measured and rewarded becomes sustainable.

When all links in the chain operate in sync, pillar scores rise, operational performance improves, and the organization moves to the next maturity stage. When any link breaks, progress stalls or reverses.

Chapter 7: Implementation—Getting Started Monday Morning

Why Role Clarity Matters More Than Motivation

I've worked with organizations where everyone was motivated to improve their sense of belonging, but nothing changed because nobody knew specifically what they were supposed to do differently. Good intentions without role clarity create activity without impact.

Role accountability eliminates the ambiguity. Executives recognize the need to integrate belonging metrics into scorecards at Stage 3. Managers recognize the importance of using pillar reports for development planning. Employees recognize the importance of taking responsibility for providing peer support and sharing knowledge.

This specificity is what distinguishes belonging infrastructure from belonging aspiration. When people understand the specific behavioral expectations in their role at their organization's maturity stage, execution becomes possible.

The Cascade Effect

What makes this behavioral chain powerful is how it cascades through the organization. When executives consistently model belonging behaviors, managers feel safer applying belonging principles with their teams. When managers create conditions that foster belonging, employees contribute more authentically and support one another more actively.

The cascade works in reverse as well. When executives discuss belonging but fail to model it, managers become skeptical about implementing belonging practices. When managers apply belonging practices inconsistently, employees become protective rather than contributive.

This is why role accountability has to be explicit and stage appropriate. Belonging scaling requires disciplined execution at every level.

Making It Sustainable

The organizations that sustain belonging gains over multiple years are the ones that embed role accountability into performance management, succession planning, and leadership development. Belonging behaviors become integral to what it means to be an effective executive, manager, or employee within their organization.

This doesn't happen automatically. It requires updating job descriptions, performance review criteria, promotion requirements, and leadership competency models to reflect the concept of belonging and accountability. When belonging becomes part of how success is defined and measured, it becomes sustainable regardless of leadership changes or operational pressures.

The behavioral chain becomes organizational capability rather than individual initiative. That's when belonging truly scales.

Governance for Sustained Implementation

Implementation succeeds in the short term through executive commitment and manager competence. It succeeds in the long term through governance structures that maintain attention and accountability regardless of leadership changes or operational pressures.

Effective belonging governance includes quarterly belonging councils that review data and recommend systemic adjustments, executive sponsors who own specific pillar outcomes, and escalation protocols when belonging metrics indicate emerging risks.

Chapter 7: Implementation—Getting Started Monday Morning

The governance is protection of organizational capability that takes years to build and can erode quickly without deliberate stewardship.

Governance That Protects Your Investment

Belonging initiatives that succeed long-term versus those that fade after initial enthusiasm: The difference is governance. Not bureaucratic oversight, but protection of organizational capability that takes years to build and can erode quickly without deliberate stewardship.

Building the Right Governance Structure

Effective belonging governance requires three distinct roles that work together:

Belonging Councils provide a cross-functional perspective and operational insight. I recommend a composition that includes cross-functional leaders, HR/People representatives, operational managers, and representatives of employee voice. Their purpose is to review pillar and composite scores, identify systemic issues, share high-performing unit practices, and make recommendations to the executive team. They typically meet quarterly, aligned with business review cycles, so belonging doesn't become disconnected from operational rhythm.

Executive Sponsors own the belonging agenda at the senior level. This is a small group of senior leaders who set annual targets and ensure belonging is integrated into corporate strategy. In high-maturity organizations, each sponsor becomes accountable for one or more pillars, ensuring specialized focus rather than diffused responsibility.

Data Stewards maintain measurement integrity and serve

as the link between data and decisions. These roles within HR analytics or PeopleOps ensure the integrity of pillar measurements, conduct audits, and update dashboards. They serve as the operational link between measurement outputs and decision-making forums.

Governance by Maturity Stage

Stage	Governance Signals	Primary Owner
Awareness	Informal sponsorship by DEI/People leads	HR Lead
Experimentation	Belonging data reviewed in pilot councils	Pilot Sponsors
Integration	Dashboards surface pillar deltas; scorecards adapted	Exec. + HR
Optimization	Predictive alerts and thresholds are active	Exec. Council
Continuous Innovation	Board visibility, ESG reporting, external benchmarking	Board / ESG Committee

Integration into Business Rhythm

The most effective governance models integrate belonging review into existing rhythms rather than creating separate, disconnected meetings. This includes belonging metrics in quarterly business reviews alongside revenue, margin, and customer KPIs. Additionally, there are monthly leader check-ins, where managers review their team's lowest pillars and share progress updates, and annual strategy cycles that incorporate belonging targets into planning, resourcing, and goal setting.

This integration normalizes belonging as part of the business conversation, reducing the risk that it gets sidelined during periods of operational pressure. When belonging metrics sit alongside financial metrics in the same meetings, leaders treat them with similar attention and urgency.

Predictive Risk Management

Governance enables the ability to anticipate what might happen next. I've helped organizations develop predictive analytics that flag potential belonging risks before they become crises.

- *Early Declines in Pillar Scores* trigger an investigation when any pillar drops more than three points in a quarter. This early warning system prevents minor problems from becoming major disruptions.
- *Change Event Risk* monitoring enables governance bodies to preplan mitigation strategies for mergers, reorganizations, leadership transitions, or technology rollouts that can trigger declines in belonging.
- *Critical Role Monitoring* tracks belonging conditions in roles with high replacement costs or strategic importance to prevent talent loss in areas that could compromise business continuity.

For example: A Stage 4 telecom company used predictive risk reviews to anticipate declines in belonging in a department scheduled for a significant system migration. They implemented a Connection and Support boost plan, preventing the 12 percent turnover spike typically seen in such projects.

Clear Escalation When Things Go Wrong

Effective governance includes clear escalation protocols when belonging metrics show acute deterioration:

- *Manager Level* involves immediate team discussions with targeted enablement actions. When problems are caught early, they can often be resolved at the team level without broader intervention.
- *Business Unit Level* escalation means councils review data, reallocate resources, or deploy specialist facilitators when manager-level intervention isn't sufficient.
- *Executive-Level* escalation occurs when belonging issues pose a threat to strategic objectives. The problem gets added to the executive agenda with a corrective plan due within one cycle.

Executive Dashboards and Alert Logic

- **Heat Maps:** Color-coded matrices for cross-unit pillar visibility.
- **Volatility Alerts:** Movement outside threshold (for example, ±3 points) triggers review.
- **Correlation Maps:** Belonging metrics aligned to revenue, risk, or satisfaction.

Alert Type	Trigger	Action
Safety drop in R&D	– 4 points	Flag for listening tour and manager coaching
Purpose stall in customer teams	No change in two cycles	Review recognition and impact framing
Support gap by region	APAC < global by 8 points	Target enablement investment

These escalation paths ensure belonging risks are treated with the same urgency as operational or financial risks. High-performing organizations segment belonging data by role level, geography, department, and tenure to enable pattern detection across friction points and strategic exposure areas. This segmentation allows for targeted intervention rather than broad-brush approaches that waste resources.

How Governance Evolves with Maturity

Belonging governance evolves as organizational maturity rises:

- *Stage 2–3* governance is more hands-on, with councils actively troubleshooting pilot initiatives and encouraging adoption. The focus is on building capability and proving value.
- *Stage 4–5* governance shifts toward innovation, focusing on benchmarking, testing new enablement methods, and continuously updating standards. The focus moves from building to optimizing and innovating.

High-maturity organizations refresh leadership enablement annually and rerun complete audits every twelve to eighteen months, even if pillar scores remain high. This maintains vigilance and signals that belonging is a nonnegotiable standard.

Connecting Governance to Financial Returns

Governance is also the structure that ensures the ROI of belonging remains visible and credible. This includes ROI tracking, where governance reviews incorporate updates on retention savings, productivity gains, and risk mitigation tied directly to pillar improvements. Additionally, public accountability is emphasized, as many Stage 5 organizations share their progress on belonging in environmental, social, and governance (ESG) reports, investor updates, or employer brand campaigns.

This visibility reinforces the value of governance internally and positions belonging as part of the organization's strategic advantage externally. When boards and investors see belonging governance, they understand it as operational capability rather than cultural aspiration.

Why Governance Is Your Preventive Maintenance

Think of belonging governance as a protective framework against organizational fragility. It protects gains you've made, prevents regression during difficult periods, and maintains capability through leadership transitions. Without governance, improvements in belonging often evaporate when attention shifts to other priorities or when operational pressures increase.

With governance, belonging becomes an embedded organizational capability that persists regardless of individual champions or temporary initiatives. The investment you make in belonging infrastructure gets protected through governance structures that maintain, measure, and continuously improve belonging conditions over time.

That's how belonging evolves from an initiative to an infrastructure to a sustainable competitive edge—through governance that treats it as seriously as any other business-critical capability.

Implementation succeeds when you embed belonging in existing business processes rather than creating separate programs.

Chapter 7: Implementation—Getting Started Monday Morning

But there's one critical application that gets overlooked in most belonging work: how this infrastructure enables authentic diversity, equity, and inclusion outcomes.

Why DEI Requires Belonging as a Prerequisite

This is where DEI initiatives usually fail. Organizations hire diverse people, run bias training, and update policies, but they don't fix the underlying systems that make inclusion work.

Harvard Business Review's research on DEI maturity confirms that companies "follow predictable stages on the DEI journey in sequence." Organizations with DEI "deeply embedded in their corporate DNA" reach a "sustainable stage" where "efforts pass stress tests"[204]—exactly the kind of auditable infrastructure that satisfies ESG requirements.

Research from Adler University reinforces this sequence: "For DEI initiatives to succeed, respect and fairness must be present. These requirements are rooted in the foundations of belonging."[205] Their findings emphasize that "people's actions and opportunities are strongly influenced by their environment," validating the systems approach to belonging infrastructure.

I've worked with companies that hit their diversity numbers but couldn't keep underrepresented talent. Their ESG reports looked great, but people kept quitting because the day-to-day experience was still exclusionary.

Adding diversity without fixing belonging actually makes

---

204 E. Washington, "The Five Stages of DEI Maturity," *Harvard Business Review*, October 31, 2022, https://hbr.org/2022/11/the-five-stages-of-dei-maturity.

205 Andrea Carter, "In the Face of DEI Backlash, Belonging Plays a Key Role to Future Success," *Adler University*, September 2, 2024, https://www.adler.edu/2024/09/03/in-the-face-of-dei-backlash-belonging-plays-a-key-role-to-future-success/.

turnover worse for underrepresented groups.[206] You're asking people to join a system that wasn't designed for them to succeed.

The bottom line: No belonging infrastructure means no sustainable DEI. You can't achieve authentic diversity, equity, and inclusion outcomes without the trust and belonging foundation that makes inclusion possible in daily operations.

DEI works when you build it on trust and belonging:

- Trust lets people have real conversations about bias and exclusion without everyone getting defensive.
- Belonging infrastructure ensures that diversity actually translates into inclusion in daily operations—in meetings, decisions, recognition, and advancement.
- DEI results happen naturally when diverse perspectives get genuinely valued and integrated into how work gets done.
- ESG credibility comes from being able to connect your social impact claims to actual measurable results through trust and belonging infrastructure.

Why DEI Initiatives Fail and How to Fix Them

Most DEI failures happen for three specific reasons, each with a direct solution:

- **Performative DEI statements without action** happen because of a lack of psychological safety. Fix it by embedding safety into meeting norms and leader feedback cycles so people can have real conversations about bias.
- **Initiative fatigue** where programs launch and die stems

---

206 L. H. Nishii, "The Benefits of Climate for Inclusion," *Academy of Management Journal* 56, no. 6 (2013): 1754–1774, https://doi.org/10.5465/amj.2009.0823.

from no structured role expectations. Use a maturity model to stage leader and employee responsibilities instead of hoping everyone figures it out.
- DEI perceived as HR-only work results from no operational ownership. Embed belonging metrics into quarterly business reviews, not just HR dashboards, so the whole organization owns the results.

Making It All Work Together

Implementation fails when belonging competes with "real work" instead of becoming part of how work gets done. The sequence that works: Get executives aligned and measure where you are (month one), train managers and integrate belonging into regular business reviews (month two), expand what's working and embed it in processes (month three). Managers make or break belonging initiatives, not executives. Measurement drives behavior—when belonging scores show up in the same meetings as revenue numbers, leaders start paying attention to both.

Implementation succeeds when belonging practices integrate with existing business processes rather than competing for attention with operational priorities. But sustainable implementation requires measurement systems that drive behavior change in real time, not annual culture surveys that provide historical data when problems have already crystallized into expensive crises.

The belonging measurement system I've developed works differently from traditional engagement tracking. It functions both as diagnostic tool and behavioral intervention. When people know psychological safety and inclusion are being measured with the same discipline as financial performance, they start creating those conditions naturally.

CHAPTER 8

Measurement That Drives Results

The belonging measurement system works in two ways: It shows you where problems exist, and it prevents new problems from forming. When people know psychological safety and inclusion are being measured, they start creating those conditions naturally.

Why Measurement Changes Everything

Measuring belonging changes behavior, not just tracks it. When belonging metrics appear in quarterly reviews alongside revenue and margin data, leaders begin to manage belonging with the same discipline they apply to financial performance. When managers receive team-level pillar reports, they start adjusting their daily activities. Check belonging quarterly for planning, monthly for adjustments, and continuously for immediate problems.[207]

Organizations that track their belonging gains measure them in the same way they measure revenue, continuously.[208] What gets measured consistently gets managed.[209] I use measurement rhythm to drive behavior change, not just track it.

Longitudinal measurement studies demonstrate that belonging conditions predict business outcomes with greater accuracy than traditional engagement surveys. Research comparing quarterly belonging assessments with annual engagement data found that belonging metrics provided a six-month warning of retention risks that engagement surveys missed entirely.[210] The predictive advantage stems from measuring structural conditions rather than emotional states—engagement reflects how people feel about past experiences, while belonging indicates whether current conditions support future contribution.

The measurement frequency effect operates through changes in manager behavior. Studies tracking team dynamics during monthly versus annual assessment cycles reveal that frequent belonging measurements create accountability loops that enhance manager responsiveness to team needs.[211] Managers who receive monthly feedback on their belonging adjust their support behaviors 3.2 times more frequently than those

---

207 BetterUp, 2024.

208 Deloitte, 2025; BetterUp, 2024.

209 R. S. Kaplan and D. P. Norton, *The Balanced Scorecard: Translating Strategy into Action* (Harvard Business School Press, 1996).

210 Sage Journals, "Predictive Validity of Belonging Measures in Organizational Settings," *Industrial and Organizational Psychology Quarterly* 47, no. 2 (2024): 156–171.

211 Schaufeli et al., 2023

who receive annual data, resulting in measurably higher team performance and lower absenteeism.

Multilevel Measurement Approach

Individual belonging problems usually signal system-level issues. Stephen Raudenbush and Anthony Bryk's research on hierarchical modeling provides the framework for understanding how individual belonging experiences aggregate into organizational patterns.[212] When someone like Alicia has a poor belonging experience, it doesn't just affect her—it reveals something about how the system treats people like her.

Tom A. B. Snijders and Roel J. Bosker's work on multilevel analysis shows how to trace team-to-individual patterns.[213] This approach predicts how changes in organizational belonging conditions will affect individual performance and retention. That's the data CFOs need to justify investment.

Here's what this looks like in practice: When Safety scores decline in engineering, you can predict which specific engineers are most likely to quit in the next six months. Not because of individual performance issues, but because the structural conditions that determine whether engineers feel safe speaking up are breaking down.

Most employee surveys treat everyone's answers as independent data points. That misses the system effects. When three people on the same team report low Connection scores, that's not three individual problems—it's one team problem that's affecting multiple people.

---

[212] S. W. Raudenbush and A. S. Bryk, *Hierarchical Linear Models: Applications and Data Analysis Methods*, 2nd ed. (Sage, 2002).

[213] T. A. B. Snijders and R. J. Bosker, *Multilevel Analysis: An Introduction to Basic and Advanced Multilevel Modeling*, 2nd ed. (Sage, 2012).

The multilevel approach turns belonging measurement from opinion polling into predictive analytics. Instead of learning that people were unhappy after they quit, you can identify system breakdowns months before they impact retention and performance.

This structural approach transforms belonging measurement from periodic sentiment tracking into business intelligence that actually drives decisions.

How Measurement Rhythm Creates Different Behaviors

The frequency of measurement determines what behaviors emerge. Here's what I've observed:

- **Annual measurement** produces year-end scrambles. Managers suddenly hold team-building sessions in November and December, hoping to influence scores. People game the survey timing, warning each other when "culture surveys" are coming. By the time results arrive, the behaviors that created problems are months old and harder to connect to specific actions.
- **Quarterly measurement** changes planning cycles. Managers start thinking about belonging conditions when they set quarterly goals. They ask different questions in their one-on-ones: "What's blocking you?" instead of just "How's the project going?" They schedule belonging check-ins the same way they schedule budget reviews.
- **Monthly pulse checks** create ongoing awareness. Teams start noticing patterns they missed before. A manager realizes that people stop contributing ideas after the

third week of each sprint cycle. Another notices that remote team members score lower on Connection during months with fewer video calls. These patterns become visible only with frequent measurement.

- **Real-time behavioral tracking** prevents problems before they escalate. When managers know that meeting participation, idea implementation rates, and cross-team collaboration are being monitored continuously, they adjust on the spot. They notice when someone hasn't spoken in three meetings. They catch themselves interrupting people. They follow up on suggestions within days instead of weeks.

What Changes When Measurement Becomes Routine?

- **Meeting behaviors shift.** When managers know that Inclusion scores track whose ideas get implemented, they start documenting who suggests what and following up on suggestions. Meetings become more structured to ensure everyone speaks before decisions are made. People stop talking over each other because they know voice equity is being measured.
- **Recognition patterns evolve.** When Purpose scores are tied to how well people understand their impact, managers start connecting individual work to broader outcomes in their feedback. Instead of saying "Good job," they say "Your analysis helped us avoid a costly mistake" or "Your design improved customer satisfaction by making the process clearer."

- **Support becomes proactive.** When managers know Support scores will be reviewed monthly, they start checking on workload before people ask for help. They schedule regular "barrier removal" sessions. They ask "What would make your job easier?" instead of waiting for complaints.
- **Connection gets intentional.** When Connection scores show up in team reports, managers create structured opportunities for relationship building. They pair people from different functions on projects. They ask about weekend plans not just to be friendly, but because they know isolated employees score lower on belonging.
- **Early warning systems activate.** Teams start noticing early signs of belonging breakdown: fewer questions in meetings, delayed responses to requests for feedback, people working longer hours without asking for help. These behaviors become signals to investigate rather than problems to ignore.

The Segmentation Effect

When belonging scores are broken down by different groups, it reveals patterns that change leadership behavior immediately.

For example: A technology company might find that their overall scores looked strong, but engineers who joined in the last six months scored twelve points lower on Psychological Safety. This prompted changes to onboarding: New engineers now get paired with "safety sponsors" who explicitly encourage questions and mistake-sharing during the first ninety days.

Another organization discovered that their Connection scores varied dramatically by floor in their office building. Teams

Chapter 8: Measurement That Drives Results

on the executive floor scored highest; teams in the basement scored lowest. This wasn't coincidence—it was proximity to leadership visibility. They redesigned office assignments and meeting locations to distribute connection opportunities more evenly.

When Measurement Drives Strategic Decisions

Advanced organizations use belonging data the same way they use financial data—to guide major business choices.

A consulting firm used belonging metrics to decide which offices could handle a major client expansion. Instead of just looking at capacity and skills, they examined psychological safety and support scores. Offices with high belonging could absorb increased pressure and new team members more effectively. Offices with low scores needed belonging infrastructure investment before taking on growth.

A healthcare system can integrate belonging data into their acquisition strategy. When evaluating potential merger targets, they can assess culture compatibility through belonging scores. Organizations with similar pillar profiles integrated more smoothly. Those with major gaps required longer integration timelines and additional resources.

The Measurement System That Works

To make belonging measurement work, it must function like any other business metric system—frequent, specific, and directly linked to the decisions leaders make.[214]

---

214 Deloitte, 2025.

Building Pillar-Level Intelligence

The five pillars—Psychological Safety, Inclusion, Support, Connection, and Purpose—each require their own measurement approach because they operate differently in practice.[215] It is essential to measure both perception (how people experience each condition) and behavior (what actually happens in meetings, processes, and daily interactions).

The measurement design matters more than most leaders realize. High-performing organizations collect pillar data on a quarterly basis, not annually. Early-stage organizations may start with twice-yearly cycles, but they increase the frequency as they mature, because belonging conditions can shift quickly during periods of change.

Question design has to be behaviorally specific.[216] Instead of asking "Do I feel included?" which can have varying meanings, we ask "Are my ideas considered when decisions are made?" Leaders can actually take action on the second one.

Segmentation reveals where belonging breaks down. Pillar scores need to be broken down by role level, department, geography, and demographic variables where appropriate. Without segmentation, you miss the patterns that matter most.[217]

When organizations implement pillar measurement with proper segmentation, they often discover that their intuitions about belonging were wrong. The departments they thought were thriving might have hidden problems. The locations they

---

[215] Achievers Workforce Institute, *The Belonging Blueprint: How to Create a Culture of Belonging for Every Worker in Your Organization* (Achievers, 2025), https://www.achievers.com/resources/white-papers/workforce-institute-belonging-blueprint/.
[216] Hagerty & Patusky, 1995.
[217] Achievers Workforce Institute. (2021). *Belonging at work report.* Achievers.

worried about might actually be doing well. The demographic groups they assumed were struggling might be the most engaged.

Composite Scores as System Health Indicators

The composite belonging score aggregates all pillar scores into a single index, providing a system-wide health overview at a glance. Composite scores work best for trend analysis—whether you're moving up or down, rather than comparing yourself to other organizations.

The fundamental insight comes from pairing composite scores with pillar variance analysis. A high composite score can mask severe weaknesses in one or two pillars, creating fragility. An organization with a composite score of 102/125 but a Connection score of 14/25 gets flagged as Stage 3, not Stage 4, because pillar consistency is required for advancement.

This is why I focus on the variance as much as the average. Uneven pillar performance creates mixed signals that confuse people about whether they belong.

Connecting Belonging to Business Outcomes

Belonging metrics have the most significant impact when they're directly tied to business KPIs that executives already track. I help organizations integrate belonging data into retention models, productivity metrics, innovation throughput, and risk indicators.

The connections are more direct than most leaders expect. Changes in pillar scores, particularly those related to Support and Purpose, correlate strongly with turnover rates in critical roles. Inclusion and Psychological Safety scores predict idea generation, approval, and implementation rates.[218] Early declines in Safety or Connection often precede increased incident reports, compliance breaches, or customer complaints.

Healthcare organizations that track psychological safety often find correlations with patient safety incidents. When staff feel safer reporting concerns, problems get caught earlier. Financial services firms see connections between inclusion practices and risk management—diverse perspectives help reveal overlooked areas that homogeneous teams miss. Manufacturing companies link connection scores to safety records—teams that trust each other look out for each other more effectively.

The operational linkage between belonging conditions and business outcomes is what gets board attention and sustained investment.

Executive Dashboards That Drive Decisions

The executive dashboard translates belonging conditions into actionable business intelligence, enabling strategic decision-making and informed resource allocation. High-maturity organizations present belonging metrics alongside financial, operational, and customer metrics in quarterly reviews, reinforcing belonging as an operational driver rather than a "people initiative."

Essential Dashboard Components:

- **Top-level:** Composite score, variance by pillar, and change since last cycle
- **Drill-down:** Heat maps by unit, function, or geography

---

218 Deloitte, 2025.

- **Predictive flags:** Alerts when a pillar's decline exceeds set thresholds, signaling need for intervention
- **ROI overlays:** Translation of belonging score changes into estimated financial impact (avoided turnover costs, productivity gains, risk mitigation value)

The dashboard combines composite scoring with pillar-specific breakdowns to show both overall belonging health and specific intervention priorities. Quarter-over-quarter change indicators reveal trending patterns, while target settings create accountability for improvement.

Executive Dashboard Key Metrics (Example)

Metric	Current	Change (QoQ)	Target	Notes
Composite Belonging Score	92/125	+4	100	Trending upward
Highest Pillar	Inclusion (21/25)	+2	22	Steady improvement
Lowest Pillar	Support (15/25)	−1	18	Needs intervention
Estimated Retention Savings	$1.2M	+$300K	$1.5M	Linked to lower attrition

Ethical Measurement

When you start measuring belonging, you're collecting data about how people experience your organization. That creates privacy problems most leaders don't think about.

Deloitte's research shows that only 27 percent of organizations have protocols for ethical data collection, despite knowing about surveillance and privacy risks.[219] People worry that belonging data might get used against them in performance reviews or promotion decisions, especially when it's unclear how the information gets used.

Hidden measurement destroys the trust that belonging is supposed to build. People need to know what you're collecting, how you're analyzing it, and who sees the results.

Four things make belonging measurement trustworthy instead of creepy: Tell people exactly what data you collect and how it affects decisions, make participation voluntary beyond basic surveys, check regularly whether your measurement accidentally excludes certain groups, and give people ways to complain about measurement problems without getting fired.

Ethical Measurement and Privacy Considerations

Privacy and Surveillance Risks

Monitoring and measurement tools (such as sentiment analysis, network mapping, or AI-driven engagement platforms) can be perceived as invasive if not transparently managed, potentially eroding trust and psychological safety among employees. Employees may fear misuse of personal or behavioral data, especially if there's ambiguity around how data informs promotion, compensation, or performance management.[220]

Governance Gaps

Deloitte's findings show that although many companies are

---

219 Deloitte, *Ethics and the Future of Human Capital Data* (Deloitte Center for Ethical Leadership, 2024).
220 Deloitte, 2025.

aware of potential pitfalls, few have formal mechanisms (leadership, policies, oversight boards) to ensure ethical data practices. Without such protocols, organizations risk accidental privacy breaches, biased decision-making, or the creation of punitive environments.

Comprehensive Ethical Framework for Belonging Infrastructure

Responsible belonging implementation requires intentional mitigation of potential downsides including privacy invasions, bias amplification, and exclusion of nonconforming individuals. Leading consulting research from Boston Consulting Group and Deloitte calls for **comprehensive ethical frameworks** that address multiple risk dimensions.

Core Ethical Principles

- **Transparent Measurement and Data Governance:** Employees must understand what data is collected, how it's analyzed, who has access, and how it influences decisions. Hidden measurement undermines the trust that belonging infrastructure aims to build.
- **Inclusive Strategy Design:** All stakeholder voices—including skeptics and cultural minorities—must be included in framework design and adaptation. Top-down belonging initiatives often perpetuate existing exclusion patterns.
- **Regular Risk Assessment and Bias Detection:** Evaluation of whether belonging measurement and interventions are creating unintended exclusion or discrimination. This

includes algorithmic bias in analytics and cultural bias in pillar interpretation.
- **Leadership Accountability Mechanisms:** Clear escalation paths, ombudsperson functions, and regular training in responsible practices. Leaders must be accountable for ethical implementation, not just belonging outcomes.

Potential Downsides and Mitigation Strategies

Privacy and Surveillance Concerns:

- *Risk:* Belonging measurement can feel invasive or create fear of retaliation.
- *Mitigation:* Voluntary participation, aggregated reporting, clear data retention policies.

Conformity Pressure:

- *Risk:* Belonging initiatives may pressure individuals to suppress authentic differences.
- *Mitigation:* Explicit celebration of productive differences, inclusion measures that value diverse perspectives.

Bias Amplification:

- *Risk:* Belonging practices may reinforce existing cultural biases about who "fits."
- *Mitigation:* Regular bias audits, diverse leadership in belonging governance, cultural adaptation processes.

Manipulation Concerns:

- *Risk:* Using belonging infrastructure to increase compliance rather than genuine engagement.
- *Mitigation:* Focus on removing barriers to authentic contribution rather than compelling specific behaviors.

Ethical Implementation Consideration

Organizations must communicate transparently about what belonging data they collect, how they analyze it, and who has access to the results. Employees should never discover measurement systems they didn't know existed. Participation in belonging assessments should remain voluntary, with no penalties for those who choose not to participate beyond basic organizational surveys.

Regular bias audits help identify whether belonging practices inadvertently favor certain groups or exclude others. These audits should examine both the measurement tools themselves and the interventions that result from belonging data. When ethical concerns arise, employees need clear paths to raise these issues without fear of retaliation, including ombudsperson roles or ethics hotlines.

Belonging governance requires diverse leadership representation to reveal overlooked areas that homogeneous leadership teams often miss. Cultural adaptation processes must respect local values and norms rather than imposing uniform practices across different cultural contexts. The focus should remain on removing structural barriers that prevent authentic contribution rather than trying to modify individual personalities or behaviors to fit predetermined belonging profiles.

These practices protect against the risk that belonging measurement itself becomes a source of surveillance anxiety or conformity pressure that undermines the trust it aims to build.

Department-Level Belonging Performance Analysis

The departmental heat map reveals how belonging conditions vary across organizational units, enabling targeted interventions and resource allocation based on specific team needs. This visualization transforms abstract concepts of belonging into actionable intelligence for managers and HR business partners.

The color-coded scoring system provides immediate visual identification of strengths and intervention priorities across all five pillars. Departments with consistent green performance (scores of 21–25) demonstrate a mature belonging infrastructure, while red areas (scores below 15) indicate structural issues requiring immediate attention. The composite scores enable leaders to prioritize support for units with the most significant improvement potential while learning from high-performing teams.

Sample Department Heat Map

Department	Psychological Safety	Inclusion	Support	Connection	Purpose & Mattering	Composite (Max 125)
Marketing	22	21	18	20	23	104
Sales	17	19	16	15	18	85
Engineering	20	18	14	13	19	84
Operations	23	22	21	22	24	112
Customer Service	15	16	13	12	17	73

Chapter 8: Measurement That Drives Results

How to Read This Heat Map

- Light grey for scores 21–25 (strong pillar performance).
- Dark grey for scores 15–20 (moderate performance; targeted improvement needed).
- Black shading for scores below 15 (priority intervention areas).

Although Marketing and Operations both have composites above 100, **Sales and Customer Service** have clear weaknesses in Support and Connection that would be hidden if leadership looked only at the average.

The heat map example illustrates why segmentation is important. Even though Marketing and Operations both have composites above 100, Sales and Customer Service have apparent weaknesses in Support and Connection that would be hidden if leadership looked only at averages. Seramount's "Measuring Belonging in the Workplace" tool kit explicitly demonstrates why segmentation across departments/levels is essential for actionable belonging measurement.[221]

High-maturity organizations present belonging metrics alongside financial, operational, and customer metrics in quarterly reviews. This colocation reinforces belonging as an operational driver rather than a "people initiative."

Wondering how to present belonging metrics to executives who think culture is "soft stuff"? The dashboard templates in Appendix C illustrate exactly how Stage 4 organizations present belonging data alongside revenue metrics in board meetings,

---

221 Seramount, 2024.

as well as the escalation protocols that prevent belonging risks from escalating into expensive crises.

How to Present to Different Executive Audiences

The same belonging data requires different presentation approaches depending on your executive audience. Frame belonging infrastructure in language that drives action.

For CEOs: Strategic Execution and Competitive Advantage

Key Messages:

- "Belonging infrastructure enables faster strategy implementation through improved coordination."
- "High-belonging teams adapt 40 percent faster during organizational change."
- "Our belonging advantage attracts top talent while competitors struggle with retention."

Dashboard Focus: cross-functional project completion rates, time-to-decision cycles, strategic initiative success rates, competitive talent attraction metrics.

For CFOs: ROI and Risk Mitigation

Key Messages:

- "Belonging improvements deliver 4:1 ROI through reduced replacement costs and productivity gains."
- "Predictive belonging analytics prevent $X million in turnover-related costs annually."

Chapter 8: Measurement That Drives Results

Dashboard Focus: retention cost savings, productivity improvement value, risk mitigation value, investment tracking with clear ROI

For CHROs: Systematic Capability
Key Messages:

- "Belonging infrastructure systematizes culture rather than depending on individual managers."
- "Measurement discipline enables data-driven culture decisions, not intuition-based programming."

Dashboard Focus: pillar-specific improvement trending, manager competency development, internal mobility success rates, employer brand correlation.

For COOs: Operational Efficiency
Key Messages:

- "High-belonging teams require 25 percent less management oversight while maintaining performance."
- "Strong belonging conditions enable early problem detection, reducing operational surprises."

Dashboard Focus: cross-team collaboration effectiveness, problem escalation speed, performance consistency during pressure periods.

For Board Members: Governance and Risk Management
Key Messages:

- "Belonging infrastructure provides a systematic approach to human capital risk management."
- "Strong belonging conditions create organizational resilience during market disruption."

Dashboard Focus: organizational resilience indicators, human capital risk assessment, ESG-relevant metrics.

Presentation Timing Guidelines

- Monthly Reviews (5–10 minutes): trending, alerts, immediate actions
- Quarterly Reviews (15–20 minutes): complete dashboard, strategic implications, resource decisions
- Board Presentations (10–15 minutes): health indicators, strategic integration, governance implications

Language That Works vs. Language That Doesn't

Use This:

- "Belonging infrastructure enables execution"
- "Data-driven culture optimization"
- "Competitive advantage through human capability"

Avoid This:

Chapter 8: Measurement That Drives Results

- "People need to feel valued" (too soft)
- "Culture transformation" (sounds disruptive)
- "Employee happiness" (not tied to business outcomes)

Handling Skepticism

- "This sounds touchy-feely": Lead with retention cost data and productivity metrics.
- "We don't have time for culture work": Reframe as "execution infrastructure that makes everything else work better."
- "People should just do their jobs": Show the cost of defensive behavior and coordination overhead.

The goal is to show executives that belonging infrastructure delivers the business outcomes they already want.

From Data to Action: The Data-to-Decision Chain

Measurement without action erodes trust faster than no measurement at all. The approach that prevents belonging metrics from becoming another unused dashboard:

1. Collect through audits or pulse measurement.
2. Interpret to identify strengths and gaps.
3. Prioritize one or two high-ROI opportunities per cycle.
4. Assign explicit accountability to specific leaders.
5. Act through targeted enablement or process changes.
6. Review to track whether changes produced intended outcomes.

Example: A Stage 2 tech company audit revealed a nine-point gap in Connection scores between engineering and marketing teams. The decision pathway: joint project squads, shared retrospectives, and cross-departmental shadowing.

Connecting Belonging to Business Outcomes

Belonging metrics gain executive attention when directly tied to business KPIs that leaders already track:

Retention Impact:

- Safety pillar decline → six-month advance warning of voluntary turnover
- Support gaps → predictable absenteeism spikes and overtime costs
- Connection breakdown → cross-functional project failure rates

Performance Impact:

- Psychological Safety scores → innovation pipeline and idea implementation rates
- Inclusion metrics → decision quality and bias-related risk exposure
- Purpose alignment → discretionary effort and goal achievement rates

Risk Management:

- Early belonging decline → compliance incidents and safety violations

- Manager competency gaps → team performance volatility
- Cultural misalignment → customer satisfaction correlation

Predictive Analytics and Early Warning Systems

Advanced belonging measurement moves from reactive to predictive:

Leading Indicators (3-6 months advance warning):

- Manager one-on-one frequency decline
- Meeting participation inequality trends
- Cross-team collaboration reduction
- Recognition distribution concentration

Risk Threshold Alerts:

- Any pillar drops >3 points in single quarter
- Department variance >10 points from organizational average
- Manager competency scores below advancement threshold
- New hire ninety-day belonging trajectory negative

Automated Escalation:

- Level 1: Team manager notification and intervention protocol

- Level 2: Department leader involvement with resource allocation
- Level 3: Executive team activation with crisis management plan

ROI Calculation Methodologies

Direct Cost Savings:

- Avoided replacement costs: (Turnover reduction %) × (Average replacement cost) × (Headcount)
- Reduced recruiting spend: (Time-to-fill improvement) × (Recruiting cost per day) × (Open positions)
- Decreased training costs: (Internal mobility increase) × (External hire training differential)

Productivity Value:

- Output improvement: (Performance increase %) × (Average salary) × (Affected employees)
- Coordination efficiency: (Manager time savings) × (Manager hourly cost) × (Management population)
- Quality improvement: (Defect reduction) × (Rework cost per defect) × (Volume)

Risk Mitigation Value:

- Compliance incident prevention: (Incident reduction) × (Average incident cost)

Chapter 8: Measurement That Drives Results

- Customer retention: (Service quality improvement) × (Customer lifetime value)
- Innovation pipeline: (Idea implementation increase) × (Revenue per implemented idea)

ROI Calculation Example: 1,000-person organization, 18% baseline turnover, $145K replacement cost:

- Six-point belonging improvement → 12% turnover (industry research)
- Sixty fewer departures × $145K = $8.7M annual savings
- Belonging investment: $800K annually
- ROI: 10.9:1

Measurement Integration: Track belonging ROI quarterly alongside other strategic investments. Include in board reporting with same analytical rigor as capital expenditure analysis.

Common Implementation Pitfalls

The data-to-action chain breaks down predictably in most organizations. Here's where leaders consistently stumble:

Analysis Paralysis: Organizations collect comprehensive belonging data but spend months debating interpretation instead of taking targeted action. The cure: Establish a thirty-day maximum from data collection to intervention launch. Directionally correct action beats delayed perfect analysis.

Executive Dashboard Theater: Belonging metrics appear in quarterly reviews and generate discussion but produce no assigned accountability or resource allocation. Leaders treat measurement as information rather than decision triggers. Fix this by requiring specific commitments and owners for every metric that misses the target.

Intervention Overload: Teams launch multiple belonging initiatives simultaneously after seeing comprehensive data, creating confusion and diluting impact. Focus ruthlessly on the lowest-scoring pillar or highest-ROI department. Success with one focused intervention builds credibility for broader work.

Measurement Without Feedback Loops: Organizations implement belonging improvements but fail to track whether interventions actually moved metrics. Always measure the same cohort before and after intervention, not different populations. Create explicit feedback cycles that connect actions to outcomes within sixty to ninety days.

Communication Gaps: Data insights remain in HR while managers responsible for execution never see pillar-specific results for their teams. Push granular data to the people who can act on it, not just executives who review it.

Why Measurement Changes Everything

When leaders see that belonging can be measured as precisely as revenue or cost, it changes the conversation entirely. Measurement provides clarity—leaders know exactly which conditions to strengthen. It creates credibility—data-driven belonging strategies pass CFO and board scrutiny. Above all, it enables control: consistent tracking allows for timely course correction before minor problems become major disruptions.[222]

The measurement system becomes the implementation system. When belonging metrics appear in the same reviews as

---

[222] Institute for Corporate Productivity (i4cp), *Strategic HR: Priorities and Predictions for 2025* (2025), https://www.i4cp.com/predictions; Deloitte, 2025.

Chapter 8: Measurement That Drives Results

financial metrics, managers start managing belonging with the same discipline they apply to budget variance. When pillar reports are released quarterly, teams begin to focus on the conditions that influence those scores.[223]

This is how belonging transitions from a cultural aspiration to an operational advantage—through measurement systems that make belonging as visible and actionable as any other business-critical capability.[224]

Integration Points with Existing Systems

Belonging succeeds when it integrates with systems that leaders already manage rather than creating parallel processes. Organizations that embed belonging into existing business infrastructure see faster adoption and more sustainable results.

- **Talent Acquisition:** Embedding belonging criteria in job descriptions, redesigning interview processes to assess belonging competencies alongside technical skills, and training hiring managers to evaluate psychological safety and inclusion behaviors during candidate interactions.
- **Performance Management:** Including belonging behaviors in performance expectations and leadership competency models, making belonging competency a requirement for advancement to management roles, and incorporating team belonging scores into manager performance evaluations.
- **Strategic Planning:** Considering belonging impact in resource allocation decisions and organizational design

---

223 Deloitte, 2025.
224 BetterUp, 2024.

changes. Before major initiatives, leaders assess how proposed changes will affect belonging conditions and build mitigation strategies accordingly.

- **Risk Management:** Using belonging metrics as early indicators for retention risk in critical roles, compliance risk through psychological safety monitoring, and operational risk through collaboration tracking. Belonging data provides three-to-six-month advance warning of potential workforce disruptions.

Quarterly Business Review Integration

Advanced organizations include belonging metrics in the same meetings where they review revenue, margins, and operational KPIs:

- Belonging composite scores appear on standard executive dashboards.
- Department-level heat maps identify intervention priorities.
- Correlation tracking links belonging improvements to business outcomes.
- Resource allocation decisions factor belonging infrastructure needs.

Strategic Decision Integration

Mature belonging infrastructure informs major business choices by providing predictive intelligence about organizational readiness and human capital capacity.

- *Reorganizations:* Assess belonging impact before

Chapter 8: Measurement That Drives Results

restructuring teams, identifying units with strong Connection and Support scores that can handle change more effectively. Teams with weak belonging foundations require additional change management resources and longer transition timelines.

- *Market Expansion:* Use belonging data to predict which units can handle growth pressure and increased collaboration requirements. Departments with high belonging scores demonstrate greater capacity for absorbing new team members and maintaining performance standards during expansion.
- *Technology Rollouts:* Plan change management based on current belonging conditions, with particular attention to Psychological Safety and Support scores. Units with strong belonging infrastructure adopt new technologies faster, while those with weak belonging require more intensive support resources.
- *Workforce Planning:* Factor belonging conditions into talent allocation decisions, succession planning, and capacity forecasting. High-belonging teams show more predictable retention patterns and higher internal mobility success rates.
- *Merger and Acquisition Planning:* Evaluate cultural compatibility through belonging assessments during due diligence, identifying integration risks before deal completion. Organizations with similar belonging profiles integrate more smoothly and preserve talent more effectively.

When belonging becomes a lens for improving existing

systems rather than an additional system to manage, adoption accelerates and sustainability increases.

Why Infrastructure Thinking Changes Everything

Belonging is infrastructure that must be built, not a program that can be implemented through training or communication. Like technology infrastructure, it requires ongoing investment, maintenance, and strategic protection. Organizations that treat belonging as a program rather than a foundational capability consistently underperform.

Infrastructure is what enables strategy to function. It's the set of conditions and systems that make every other initiative—whether it's a market expansion, a merger, a digital transformation, or a process improvement—more likely to succeed. When belonging operates as infrastructure, it is designed into how work gets done, rather than being added on top of it. It gets maintained and upgraded like any other core asset. Most important, it becomes a prerequisite for execution rather than a discretionary "culture" project.

Belonging as Your Design Filter

Infrastructure thinking starts at the design phase. Belonging becomes a decision filter when creating or revising systems, policies, and workflows.

Here's how this works in practice:

- *Talent acquisition* gets redesigned with belonging as a core requirement. Job descriptions are reviewed for inclusive language and realistic requirements. Interview processes are structured to minimize bias and ensure candidates experience psychological safety during assessment. The hiring process becomes belonging infrastructure rather than just a selection mechanism.

- *Process design* involves teams cocreating standard operating procedures to ensure everyone understands their role, reducing ambiguity and increasing accountability. Instead of top-down procedure manuals, you get collaborative design that fosters belonging throughout your workflow.
- *Technology rollouts* include communication and training plans tailored to diverse user groups, ensuring inclusion in adoption and reducing resistance. Belonging-driven design minimizes the friction that occurs when systems unintentionally create barriers to participation or erode trust.

The difference is that belonging becomes embedded in system design rather than being something people have to navigate around or compensate for.

Integration into Strategic Initiatives

In later stages of maturity, I've seen organizations build belonging into every major strategic initiative rather than treating it as a separate consideration.

Mergers & Acquisitions start with belonging assessment. Integration teams measure belonging conditions in both legacy organizations, identify high- and low-scoring pillars, and use that data to guide the sequencing of integrations. Instead of hoping culture integration works out, you have data to drive decisions.

Reorganizations begin with belonging impact assessment. Before restructuring teams, leaders assess Connection and Support scores to predict where trust and collaboration are at risk, allowing preventive actions rather than damage control.

Market expansions utilize regional pillar scores to inform location-specific onboarding and leadership training, thereby accelerating cultural alignment in new markets rather than assuming a one-size-fits-all approach.

Here's a concrete example: A Stage 4 logistics company can use belonging data in an acquisition to identify that Inclusion scores were significantly higher in the acquired company. Instead of imposing their existing culture, they can retain and scale the acquired firm's inclusion practices across the enterprise, avoiding the cultural "flattening" that often erodes value post-merger.

The Operational Returns

When belonging operates as infrastructure, the operational benefits show up in ways that directly affect business performance:

Execution speed increases because high-belonging environments require less managerial oversight to coordinate action. People self-organize more effectively when trust infrastructure is strong.

Decision quality improves because inclusive processes produce decisions with broader buy-in and fewer downstream reversals. When people trust that their input matters, they contribute better information and support implementation more actively.

Adaptability accelerates because teams in high-belonging cultures adjust to changes faster. They have a higher baseline

Chapter 8: Measurement That Drives Results

trust, which means they interpret change as an organizational adaptation rather than a personal threat.

These benefits appear directly in your operational metrics: cycle times, project completion rates, and change success.

Maintenance and Upgrades Are Required

Here's something most leaders overlook: Infrastructure requires ongoing maintenance. Once belonging is embedded, you must maintain and update it like any other system. This is an ongoing operational discipline.

Routine measurement through pulse checks detects early deterioration before it becomes a crisis. You run "system checks" in the same way you monitor IT systems or the health of your supply chain.

Leader enablement refresh cycles ensure skills and behaviors don't erode over time. Belonging practices require reinforcement, especially during times of leadership transition or high-pressure periods.

Standard updates reflect new research, shifting workforce demographics, and evolving strategic priorities. Belonging infrastructure that stays static becomes obsolete.

Organizations at Stage 5 run belonging system checks quarterly, not annually, treating belonging as critical to operational stability as their technology infrastructure or supply chain.

How Infrastructure Maturity Evolves

Belonging as infrastructure becomes most visible as organizations advance through maturity stages:

- *Stage 3 (Integration):* Belonging principles are applied to core processes and selected strategic projects. You start embedding belonging considerations into major decisions rather than treating them as separate initiatives.

- *Stage 4 (Optimization):* Belonging is embedded in all major change initiatives, with data driving sequencing and risk management. Belonging impact assessment becomes standard practice for strategic planning.
- *Stage 5 (Continuous Innovation):* The belonging infrastructure itself evolves in response to new challenges, opportunities, and research, ensuring it remains a strategic differentiator rather than becoming organizational overhead.

Why This Changes Your Business Case

Understanding belonging as infrastructure completely changes how you justify investment and measure returns. Instead of competing for budget against other "culture" projects, belonging becomes the following:

- A *risk-reduction strategy* that lowers the odds of failed change initiatives. When you can predict and mitigate belonging risks, strategic initiatives succeed more consistently.
- A *performance multiplier* that increases the yield of every other investment. Strong belonging infrastructure makes everything else work better—technology adoption, process improvement, market expansion, talent development.
- A *strategic differentiator* that makes culture a market-facing advantage in talent attraction, brand positioning, and

customer experience. Belonging infrastructure becomes visible to external stakeholders as operational excellence.

The Integration Reality

Belonging infrastructure either gets built intentionally or develops accidentally. When it develops unintentionally, it typically includes gaps, inconsistencies, and failure points that create operational risks.

When it gets built intentionally, using the frameworks and measurement systems we've discussed, it becomes a genuine market differentiator that compounds over time. The choice is whether to design and maintain belonging infrastructure or let it drift and hope for the best.

Infrastructure for belonging makes every other strategic initiative more likely to succeed. That's why treating it as infrastructure rather than an initiative is a strategic necessity.

Measurement discipline changes everything when belonging metrics appear in quarterly business reviews alongside revenue and margin data. Leaders start managing culture with the same attention they apply to other performance drivers. But all the measurement and improvement in the world fail without the foundational element that makes everything else possible.

That foundation is trust. What I learned after twenty years of organizational work: Trust isn't the outcome of good belonging practices, it's the prerequisite that determines whether belonging practices will work at all. Get this sequence wrong, and even the most sophisticated culture initiatives become compliance theater that changes nothing.

CHAPTER 9

Trust as the Foundation of Everything

I used to think trust was the outcome of good leadership. After years of working with teams that performed at extraordinary levels and others that couldn't execute basic coordination, I've learned the opposite is true: Trust is the foundation that makes good leadership possible.

Trust comes first. It enables belonging infrastructure, which enables authentic DEI results. This sequence gives you proof that auditors and investors can verify. Get the sequence wrong, and even well-intentioned initiatives fail. Get it right, and transformation happens two to three times faster than most leaders predict, while satisfying board-level scrutiny.

Trust Comes First, Everything Else Follows

Most organizations approach culture change backward. They launch DEI initiatives hoping to build inclusion, implement belonging programs hoping to improve retention, and wonder why trust never materializes.

The sequence that works:

1. **Trust as Foundation:** The prerequisite that enables psychological safety, authentic communication, and vulnerability without penalty.
2. **Belonging as Infrastructure:** The conditions (Safety, Inclusion, Support, Connection, Purpose) that operate as organizational infrastructure, built on trust and embedded in how work gets done.
3. **Strategic Outcomes:** Belonging infrastructure generates the data that makes your social impact claims believable.
4. **ESG as Market Position:** The environmental, social, and governance credibility that results from auditable trust and belonging infrastructure supporting measurable business outcomes.

Research from the American Society for Microbiology confirms this sequence: Trust is "defined by integrity, benevolence and ability" and requires "vulnerability and is usually a radical shift from business as usual." The study demonstrates that "information-sharing, culture change and broader institutional innovation are mediated by trust."[225]

This sequence works repeatedly. Initiatives fail when organizations skip foundational layers or treat belonging as a program instead of infrastructure.

---

[225] American Society for Microbiology, *ASM Ethics: Upholding Trust, Integrity, and Innovation in Science* (2023), https://asm.org/asm-ethics.

Chapter 9: Trust as the Foundation of Everything

How Norms Create Belonging

Most belonging initiatives fail because they focus on feelings instead of the systems that create those feelings. Belonging doesn't come from wanting people to feel included—it comes from predictable norms that signal who fits and how.

When working on the Voice of the Employee initiative, we discovered that trust issues were undermining organizational performance across multiple teams. After meeting with our chief operating officer (COO), we realized the core problem wasn't individual behavior; it was a fundamental lack of clear norms, including at the leadership level. Without predictable patterns of behavior that people could count on, trust couldn't develop, and belonging remained fragile.

Norms define what behaviors, language, and values are accepted in your organization. When people understand these norms and can align with them, they experience belonging— they feel like "one of us." When norms are unclear, inconsistent, or missing entirely, people spend mental energy trying to figure out whether they fit instead of focusing on contribution.

Think about Alicia again. She couldn't predict whether her technical suggestions would be welcomed or ignored. The norms around how ideas get evaluated weren't clear, so she had to guess whether speaking up would help or hurt her standing. That uncertainty made belonging impossible.

How Norms Signal Membership

People who follow group norms get viewed—by others and by themselves—as legitimate members. When someone adopts the behaviors, values, and rituals that matter to the group, they both feel and get recognized as insiders. This creates belonging through demonstrated membership rather than declared inclusion.

When evaluating the challenges with trust after the significant reduction in force (RIF), we learned that leaders assumed everyone understood the unwritten rules about how decisions were made, how communication flowed, and how conflicts were resolved. But those assumptions created chaos rather than clarity. People couldn't develop trust in the system because they couldn't predict how the system actually worked.

The relationship works both ways. When people feel they belong, they become more motivated to learn and follow the norms that created that belonging. This creates the virtuous cycle that makes belonging infrastructure sustainable.

Why Clear Norms Reduce Belonging Anxiety

When norms are clear, shared, and consistently applied, people feel secure in their membership because they know how to succeed. Ambiguous or shifting norms create anxiety, especially for people who are already questioning whether they fit.

For belonging to work across differences, norms must make space for individual expression while maintaining group coherence. This means having explicit norms about inclusion—how different perspectives get heard, how conflicts get resolved, how decisions incorporate diverse viewpoints.

Connecting Norms to Belonging Infrastructure

Each belonging pillar requires specific norms to function:

- **Safety norms** define how bad news is shared, how

mistakes are handled, and what happens when people speak up with problems.
- **Inclusion norms** establish whose voices are heard, how different perspectives influence decisions, and how diverse ideas are integrated.
- **Support norms** determine how help is requested and provided, how development opportunities are allocated, and how capacity is managed.
- **Connection norms** govern how relationships form across departments, how collaboration happens, and how people build trust.
- **Purpose norms** connect daily work to mission, show how values translate into decisions, and maintain alignment during change.

Without clear norms in these areas, belonging remains fragile because people can't predict whether the conditions that made them feel included will continue.

The research shows that perceived alignment with norms matters more for belonging than actual similarity. Employees require feeling that they can engage with the group's expectations while being accepted for who they are. Organizations that build belonging infrastructure create norms that enable this dual requirement—coherence and inclusion.

Why Trust Must Come First

Trust comes first. Without it, people go into self-protection mode—they hide problems, avoid risks, and focus on survival instead of contribution. Trust requires three things: People need to believe you're competent, that you care about them, and that you'll do what you say.[226]

Bridge & Rhino's neuroscience research demonstrates the business case: "Organizations that embed trust into their leadership DNA outperform competitors by up to 286 percent in terms of employee engagement, innovation, and financial performance." Their findings confirm the neurochemical mechanisms at work: "Oxytocin (trust molecule) vs. cortisol (stress hormone)" explains why trust directly affects cognitive performance and collaboration.[227]

When trust breaks down, through layoffs, leadership changes, or integrity violations, repair becomes essential. Eberl, Geiger, and Aßländer's[228] research on organizational trust repair shows that rebuilding requires acknowledging specific failures, demonstrating changed behavior consistently, and creating structural accountability that prevents future violations. Kramer and Lewicki's[229] twenty-year review confirms that trust repair follows predictable stages and requires six to eighteen months of consistent action to restore psychological safety and collaboration effectiveness.

---

226 Mayer et al., 1995.

227 Bridge & Rhino, "Leading with the Brain in Mind: The Neuroscience of Trust and Collaboration," March 16, 2025, https://bridgeandrhino.com/articles/leading-with-the-brain-in-mind-the-neuroscience-of-trust-and-collaboration/.

228 Eberl, Geiger, and Aßländer's, 2015.

229 R. M. Kramer and R. J. Lewicki, "Trust Repair in Organizations: Twenty Years of Progress and Future Directions," *Annual Review of Organizational Psychology and Organizational Behavior* 8 (2021): 259–283, https://doi.org/10.1146/annurev-orgpsych-012420-083025.

Trust Recovery: When Organizations Need to Rebuild

Trust breakdowns are inevitable—layoffs, leadership failures, policy changes that feel like betrayals. The question is whether you'll recover from a trust crisis quickly or spend years rebuilding.

Kramer & Lewicki's analysis[230] shows that organizations with solid relationship foundations bounce back from crises three times faster than those scrambling to build trust while everything's falling apart.

The Six-Step Recovery Framework

1. **Immediately Acknowledge and Take Ownership.** Leadership must acknowledge the failure publicly within twenty-four to seventy-two hours, admit what happened, express regret, and communicate the plan for investigation and recovery.[231] Leaders must take clear responsibility without defensiveness, minimization, or deflection.

2. **Employ Radical Transparency in Communication.** Be radically transparent by clearly explaining what is known and unknown, express the reasons for decisions, and set expectations for what comes next. Vague statements rebuild nothing—people need specifics to trust again.

3. **Cocreate Solutions.** Invite team input by including stakeholders in diagnosing what went wrong and in

---

230 Kramer & Lewicki, 2021.
231 Results Washington, "Crisis Communication: Leadership Steps for Transparency and Accountability" (2019), https://results.wa.gov/.

shaping recovery plans, reinforcing their agency and value. Encourage questions and emotional honesty, acknowledging pain, anger, or fear rather than rushing to "move on."

4. **Make Structural Changes.** Implement reforms and track progress by making structural changes like process updates, new norms, and reporting controls, sharing regular updates on progress and unresolved issues.[232] Show new behavior in old situations—the real test is how leaders act when similar challenges arise again.

5. **Track and Report Progress.** Measure and report using both "hard" outcome data like retention and engagement and "soft" indicators including employee sentiment and speaking-up rates.[233] Regular transparency accelerates trust rebuilding.

6. **Sustain Empathy and Presence.** Support survivors and check in regularly, rebuilding relationships through meaningful one-on-ones and acknowledging the ongoing emotional impact of disruption. Recovery takes time—resist pressure to "move on" before trust is actually rebuilt.

---

232 Queensland Public Sector Commission, *Leadership Competencies for Queensland Framework* (Brisbane, Australia: Queensland Government, 2019), https://www.forgov.qld.gov.au/leadership-competencies-queensland.

233 Federal Emergency Management Agency (FEMA), "Lesson 4: Building and Rebuilding Trust," in *Leadership and Influence (IS-240.b) Student Manual*, 4.1–4.24 (FEMA Emergency Management Institute, 2019), https://training.fema.gov/emiweb/is/is240b/sm%20files/sm_04.pdf.

Ethical Trust Building

Trust building itself raises ethical considerations, particularly around the potential for emotional manipulation or coercive culture change. The line between creating positive workplace conditions and manipulating employee emotions can be thin.

Ethical trust building focuses on removing barriers to authentic contribution rather than compelling specific emotional responses. This means creating structural conditions where people can choose to engage fully, rather than using psychological techniques to generate compliance or enthusiasm."

Why Some Organizations Never Recover

Organizations that treat trust recovery as a communication problem rather than a relationship problem stay broken. Third-party or cross-functional audits can build credibility and break down internal silos or skepticism.[234]

The organizations that recover fastest use crisis as an opportunity to build stronger trust infrastructure than existed before, turning breakdown into breakthrough.

When people feel excluded or uncertain, their brains treat it like physical injury. The part of their brain that handles complex thinking and creativity gets hijacked by survival circuits.

Brain scans show social rejection activates the same regions as physical pain.[235] When people don't trust their environment,

---

[234] Washington State Auditor's Office, *Assessing Workplace Culture at the Department of Fish and Wildlife: Executive Summary and Audit Report* (Olympia, WA: Office of the Washington State Auditor, 2019), https://sao.wa.gov/sites/default/files/audit_reports/PA_DFW_Workplace_Culture_ar-1028973.pdf.

[235] N. I. Eisenberger and M. D. Lieberman, "Why Rejection Hurts: A Common Neural Alarm System for Physical and Social Pain," *Trends in Cognitive Sciences* 8, no. 7 (2004): 294–300, https://doi.org/10.1016/j.tics.2004.05.010.

their mental energy goes to watching for threats instead of doing good work.

Google's Project Aristotle confirmed this at scale, finding that "the number one predictor of a high-performing team was psychological safety," which requires trust as its foundation.[236]

Consider Alicia's situation. Her brain was constantly scanning for social threats: Will my ideas be ignored again? Am I fitting in? That cognitive energy should have been focused on solving problems and improving processes.

Boards should care about this because low trust creates measurable business risk. Organizations with trust problems face predictable costs: Decisions take longer, innovation slows down, people quit more often, and coordination becomes expensive.

You can't build psychological safety when people don't trust each other. You can't create inclusion when people are protecting themselves. You can't establish belonging when relationships feel dangerous.

How Trust Enables Belonging Infrastructure

Each pillar needs trust as its foundation, but you have to build belonging into how work actually gets done:

1 **Psychological Safety:** People need to trust that speaking up won't hurt their career. Build safe escalation processes, structure feedback systems, and hold leaders accountable for how they respond to bad news.
2 **Inclusion:** People need to trust that their input actually

---

236 Google re:Work, *Understand Team Effectiveness: Guide: Understand Team Effectiveness* (2016), https://rework.withgoogle.com/intl/en/guides/understanding-team-effectiveness.

matters. Create decision processes that require diverse perspectives, track whose ideas get implemented, and measure whether everyone gets heard. Track whether suggestions like Alicia's get documented, evaluated, and responded to.

3. **Support:** People need to trust that help will be there when they need it. Train managers to check on workload proactively, make development accessible, and manage capacity before people burn out.
4. **Connection:** People need to trust that relationships work both ways. Create structured opportunities for people to build relationships across departments and hold leaders accountable for relationship building.
5. **Purpose:** People need to trust that the mission is real. Show clearly how each role connects to impact, communicate wins consistently, and make sure your actions match your values.

Without trust, belonging becomes checkbox compliance instead of how work gets done. When auditors and investors look at your ESG claims, they can spot the difference between real infrastructure and pretty programs.

Trust recovery research provides specific protocols for rebuilding infrastructure. Kramer and Lewicki's (2021) longitudinal analysis of organizational trust breakdowns found that systematic recovery approaches—combining acknowledgment, transparency, and structural changes—restore psychological safety 60 percent faster than communication-only interventions.[237] Organizations that follow structured trust recovery protocols report a restored belonging score within six to twelve months, while those relying solely on leadership messaging often require eighteen to twenty-four months for equivalent recovery.

The trust-belonging relationship operates through predictable neurochemical pathways. Research measuring oxytocin levels in high-trust work environments reveals that consistent leader reliability behaviors—such as following through on commitments, admitting mistakes, and providing promised resources—lead to measurable increases in cooperation and risk-taking behaviors.[238] These biological responses translate directly into operational outcomes: teams with high leader trust scores collaborate 40 percent more effectively on cross-functional projects and identify problems 60 percent faster than their low-trust counterparts.

Trust as Your Foundation

Trust is the essential organizational foundation that enables adaptability, resilience, and high performance—especially during periods of external pressure or change. When trust is strong, organizations can rapidly implement new belonging frameworks, adjust to evolving workforce expectations, deliver credible DEI outcomes, and confidently satisfy increasing ESG scrutiny from regulators and investors.

---

237 Kramer and Lewicki, 2021.
238 Zak, 2017.

Why Trust Is Foundational

- **Adaptability:** Organizations with high trust respond quickly to market shifts, disruptions, or crises. Low-trust environments become paralyzed by suspicion and self-protection, causing slow reaction times and operational breakdowns.[239]
- **Sustained Performance Under Stress:** Research shows high-trust organizations maintain operational integrity and team cohesion during uncertainty, while low-trust organizations experience fragmentation and loss of focus.[240]
- **Strategic Differentiation:** Trust infrastructure facilitates internal change like scaling belonging and DEI, while making social responsibility claims credible and verifiable to external stakeholders.[241]
- **Organizational Resilience:** Trust acts as a buffer, mitigating the negative impacts of disruptions such as market crashes, regulatory changes, or competitive pressure. Organizations with strong trust adapt quickly instead of scrambling when the unexpected hits.[242]

---

[239] Crisis Response Improvement Strategy (CRIS) Committee, *Recommendations for Behavioral Health Crisis Response in Washington* (Results Washington, 2019), https://results.wa.gov/.

[240] University of Queensland, *Leadership for Uncertain Times: Building Trust and Resilience in Organizations* (Brisbane, Australia: University of Queensland Business School, 2019).

[241] B. Temkin, "It's Time to (Re)Build Trust," *Humanity at Scale*, April 14, 2024, https://humanityatscale.substack.com/p/its-time-to-rebuild-trust.

[242] Sutcliffe & Vogus, 2003.

Board Implications

Boards should treat trust as a strategic asset that underpins belonging, DEI, and ESG systems. Oversight must go beyond culture surveys to assess whether management has built trust infrastructure that can withstand stress, scrutiny, and unplanned challenges.[243]

Organizations with solid trust can build belonging systems quickly when workforce expectations change, deliver real DEI results when regulations tighten, and back up their ESG claims when investors start asking hard questions. High-trust organizations maintain performance during uncertainty while low-trust systems fragment under pressure.

What Boards Need to Know

Boards should view trust and belonging as core business capabilities that affect long-term value and risk.

Smart boards can provide real oversight instead of just checking compliance boxes. They can judge management on whether they're actually building sustainable systems, not just running annual culture surveys. They can evaluate ESG claims based on what auditors can verify, not what sounds good in reports.

The real question for boards is whether they're building trust and belonging systems that can survive external scrutiny and operational pressure.

Making Trust Operational

Trust becomes real when you measure it like revenue and

---

[243] Your Thought Partner, *Trust as Strategic Infrastructure: Board Oversight for ESG, DEI, and Belonging* (2023), https://yourthoughtpartner.com/.

Chapter 9: Trust as the Foundation of Everything

manage it through specific practices, not hope that people will just get along.

- **Measure trust through hard numbers:** retention rates, internal promotions, cross-functional project success, and innovation rates. Also track softer signals: who speaks up in meetings, how quickly problems get escalated, and how well teams collaborate across departments.
- **Build trust through consistent actions:** transparent decisions, following through on commitments, communicating clearly during tough times, and holding people accountable when they mess up.

Trust gets built through what you do, not what you say.[244] People watch how leaders handle difficult situations, not how they sound in all-hands meetings.

This operational approach gives boards real oversight instead of just checking boxes. It provides predictive indicators for strategic planning instead of backward-looking culture surveys.

Trust makes everything else work. Build belonging on solid trust and your DEI results become authentic instead of performative. Skip the trust foundation and your belonging work becomes expensive compliance theater that wastes time and money while changing nothing.

When McDonald's faced derivative lawsuits over culture failures, or when Amazon required federal intervention for workplace conditions, these weren't just HR problems—they were failures of oversight that created legal and financial exposure

---

244 Schein, 1985.

for executives and boards. The ESG landscape is shifting toward accountability, and belonging infrastructure provides the auditable foundation that transforms social responsibility from marketing copy into measurable competitive advantage.

CHAPTER 10

Making Social Impact Auditable—ESG and Belonging Infrastructure

The ESG Credibility Crisis

In 2023, McDonald's faced a derivative lawsuit alleging that the former head of human resources breached his fiduciary duties by consciously ignoring red flags regarding sexual harassment and misconduct at the company. Despite public ESG commitments to workplace culture and employee well-being, internal evidence suggested failures in human capital oversight. Though it was dismissed, the Delaware Court of Chancery's ruling—that oversight duties extend to corporate officers, not just directors—sent shock waves through executive suites as a "wake-up call" for corporate leaders who had treated culture as a compliance checkbox rather than operational infrastructure.

Organizations across industries make bold ESG commitments backed by aspirational statements and diversity statistics, only to face credibility crises when the underlying human capital infrastructure fails. Boston Consulting Group's analysis of more than twenty-seven thousand employees across sixteen countries found that companies increasing their inclusion measurement from the lowest quartile to the median can "slash attrition risk by 50 percent." The study revealed that "when senior leaders are committed to DEI, 84 percent of their employees feel valued and respected, as opposed to 44 percent in companies where leaders are not viewed as committed."[245]

The problem is the lack of auditable evidence supporting claims. Amazon required federal intervention through a Department of Labor settlement mandating "corporate-wide ergonomic measures at facilities across the country" after workplace safety failures. Uber faced scrutiny over workplace harassment and toxic culture despite public diversity commitments. Apple confronted renewed criticism for supplier labor conditions involving excessive hours and poor working conditions.

Deloitte's research on ESG market value shows that "a 10-point difference in an ESG score is associated with an approximate 1.2x higher EV/EBITDA multiple," yet "investors are increasingly relying on ESG disclosures to make important decisions . . . yet remain dissatisfied with the level of appropriate quantitative ESG information."[246] Only 29 percent of

---

[245] Boston Consulting Group (BCG), "Leadership That Prioritizes Inclusion in the Workplace Can Slash Attrition Risk," February 21, 2023, https://www.bcg.com/press/22february2023-leadership-that-prioritizes-inclusion-can-slash-attrition-risk.

[246] Deloitte, *Does a Company's ESG Score Have a Measurable Impact on Its Market Value?* (2023), https://www.deloitte.com/ch/en/services/consulting-financial/research/does-a-company-esg-score-have-a-measurable-impact-on-its-market-value.html.

Chapter 10: Making Social Impact Auditable—ESG and Belonging Infrastructure

S&P reporting companies obtained external assurance on their sustainability information as of 2019.

ESG frameworks increasingly demand proof, not promises. Investors, regulators, and stakeholders want measurable evidence that social responsibility commitments translate into operational reality. Traditional culture surveys and demographic data provide snapshots, but they can't demonstrate the conditions that create sustainable human capital outcomes.

Belonging infrastructure solves this credibility gap by providing the measurable foundation that ESG frameworks require. Instead of relying on periodic surveys or demographic data, belonging metrics track the ongoing conditions that produce the outcomes ESG stakeholders care about: retention, voice, collaboration, innovation, and equity.

When ESG claims are built on documented belonging infrastructure, they become verifiable rather than aspirational. External auditors can trace social impact claims back through specific systems and metrics rather than accepting statements of intent.

Why ESG Statements Become Liabilities

Organizations face board-level scrutiny when their ESG claims about workplace culture can't withstand examination. Diversity metrics without belonging infrastructure evidence. Inclusion statements without trust measurement data. Social sustainability claims without support allocation processes.

When external stakeholders examine ESG commitments closely, they're looking for evidence, not aspirational language. Without trust and belonging infrastructure, ESG positioning becomes a liability instead of an advantage.

The Board-Level Business Case

For board members evaluating human capital strategy, the infrastructure approach provides both risk mitigation and competitive positioning:

- *Risk Mitigation:* Trust and belonging infrastructure reduces exposure to culture-related crises, talent exodus, innovation stagnation, and reputation damage that affect shareholder value.

- *Strategic Positioning:* Organizations with auditable trust and belonging infrastructure can credibly compete for ESG-focused investment, top-tier talent, and customers who evaluate supplier social responsibility.

- *Regulatory Readiness:* As human capital disclosure requirements expand, infrastructure-based approaches provide the data that compliance frameworks increasingly require.

Boards shouldn't ask whether culture matters. They should ask whether management is building auditable culture infrastructure sustainable under external scrutiny.

What ESG Frameworks Actually Require

ESG reporting frameworks—whether SEC human capital disclosures, GRI standards, or SASB metrics—increasingly focus on evidence rather than programmatic statements. Understanding what auditors actually look for helps organizations build the right measurement infrastructure.

Human Capital Disclosures

- Workforce stability metrics that predict business continuity risk.
- Talent development systems with measurable advancement outcomes.
- Leadership effectiveness indicators tied to team performance.
- Systematic approaches to knowledge retention and transfer.

Workforce Health & Engagement Metrics

- Early warning systems for burnout, stress, and performance degradation.
- Voice mechanisms that demonstrate psychological safety in practice.
- Response protocols that show how feedback translates into organizational action.
- Support allocation systems that prevent predictable workforce disruptions.

Social Cohesion Evidence

- Cross-functional collaboration rates that enable strategic execution.
- Trust indicators that correlate with operational efficiency.
- Inclusion processes that produce measurable equity outcomes.

- Connection patterns that predict retention and performance stability.

Risk Management Integration

- Human capital risk factors integrated into enterprise risk assessment.
- Predictive indicators that provide advance warning of workforce disruptions.
- Intervention protocols that prevent escalation of people-related risks.
- Correlation tracking between workforce conditions and business outcomes.

The shift from aspirational to operational means ESG auditors now examine the systems that create outcomes, not just the outcomes themselves. They want to see measurement discipline, intervention protocols, and improvement—the infrastructure that makes social impact sustainable rather than accidental.

A 2023 Northeastern University study of more than thirty experts found that the "HR function appears relatively unprepared for new reporting requirements" while "ESG and investor relations leaders typically do not have deep understanding of firm's human capital measurement." The research identified that "external reporting frameworks lack agreement on best ways for companies to measure and tell their human capital story."[247]

---

[247] C. Palus and T. McMullen, *Human Capital Measurement and Reporting: The New Imperative for HR and Investor Relations* (Center for Workforce Analytics, Northeastern University, 2023), https://cps.northeastern.edu/wp-content/uploads/2023/01/Human-Capital-Measurement-and-Reporting.pdf.

Belonging Metrics That Satisfy Auditors

Belonging infrastructure provides exactly the evidence ESG frameworks require. The five pillars translate into auditable metrics that demonstrate operational social responsibility:

1 Psychological Safety → Retention Correlation

- Feedback frequency: frequency and distribution of idea-sharing, concern-raising, and feedback provision across different employee groups.
- Safe escalation processes: documented protocols for raising difficult issues, with tracked response times and resolution outcomes.
- Manager trust indices: team-level measurement of psychological safety with correlation to retention and performance data.
- Innovation pipeline data: idea submission, evaluation, and implementation rates that demonstrate inclusive innovation processes.

ESG Application: Retention predictions six months in advance based on psychological safety decline, enabling proactive intervention rather than reactive damage control.

2 Support Systems → Burnout Prevention

- Workload distribution analysis: monitoring of work allocation patterns to identify and prevent unsustainable demands.

- Barrier removal tracking: documentation of obstacles identified and eliminated, with time-to-resolution metrics.
- Resource allocation equity: measurement of support resource distribution across different teams and employee groups.
- Early intervention protocols: identification and response to signs of stress or performance decline.

ESG Application: Predictive analytics that identify burnout risk three to four months before manifestation, with documented intervention success rates.

3 Connection Metrics → Collaboration Outcomes

- Cross-functional project completion rates: measurement of collaboration effectiveness across organizational boundaries.
- Knowledge sharing patterns: tracking of information flow and collaborative problem-solving across teams.
- Relationship density mapping: measurement of professional connection strength and distribution.
- Isolation identification systems: early detection of employees becoming disconnected from collaborative networks.

ESG Application: Collaboration effectiveness metrics that correlate with strategic initiative success rates and operational efficiency gains.

5 Inclusion Processes → Decision Quality

- Voice equity measurement: tracking whose ideas are heard, considered, and implemented across different decision processes.
- Bias detection systems: identification of decision-making patterns that exclude relevant perspectives.
- Diverse perspective integration: measurement of how different viewpoints influence final decisions and outcomes.
- Representation tracking: monitoring of participation patterns in high-stakes decisions and strategic planning.

ESG Application: Decision quality improvements and reduced risk exposure through inclusion of diverse perspectives.

5 Purpose Alignment → Discretionary Effort

- Impact connection measurement: tracking how well employees understand their contribution to organizational outcomes.
- Goal alignment assessment: measurement of individual purpose connection to organizational mission.
- Meaning-making support: documentation of efforts to help employees connect their work to broader impact.
- Engagement sustainability: measurement of sustained motivation and commitment.

ESG Application: Productivity and innovation metrics tied to purpose alignment, demonstrating social sustainability through workforce engagement.

The Boston Consulting Group's BLISS Index study demonstrates this approach in practice, using "statistical modeling techniques to identify workplace factors that drive feelings of inclusion" and providing "deep analytical proof that inclusion directly affects the decisions people make about their jobs."[248]

ESG Readiness by Maturity Stage

ESG credibility depends entirely on belonging infrastructure maturity. External stakeholders can easily distinguish between organizations with foundations and those making aspirational claims.

Stage 1: Awareness—Crisis Response

ESG Profile: Ad hoc statements with no supporting measurement infrastructure. ESG reports rely on diversity statistics and employee survey snapshots without evidence of underlying conditions.

Auditor Perspective: Sees through superficial claims immediately. No correlation between ESG statements and operational reality. High risk of credibility breakdown under scrutiny.

Typical ESG Content: "We value diversity and inclusion" backed by demographic data and annual survey scores without evidence of inclusive practices or belonging infrastructure.

Stage 2: Experimentation—Program Implementation

ESG Profile: Active DEI programs and culture initiatives, but metrics remain disconnected from business dashboards and

---

248 Boston Consulting Group (BCG), *Inclusion Isn't Just Nice. It's Necessary.* (2023), https://www.bcg.com/publications/2023/how-to-improve-inclusion-in-the-workplace.

strategic decision-making. Belonging efforts exist but aren't integrated into operational management.

Auditor Perspective: Recognizes genuine effort but notes lack of integration. Programs may be effective but don't demonstrate scalable infrastructure or predictable outcomes.

Typical ESG Content: Training completion rates, program participation metrics, and improved survey scores, but limited evidence of conditions that sustain outcomes.

Stage 3: Integration—Operational Embedding

ESG Profile: Belonging metrics embedded in quarterly business reviews and leadership scorecards. Clear correlation between belonging conditions and business outcomes. Measurement with management accountability.

Auditor Perspective: Finds auditable evidence of approaches. Can trace ESG claims back to operational processes and measurement systems. Credible foundation for social impact statements.

Typical ESG Content: Belonging-retention correlation data, predictive analytics for workforce stability, manager accountability for team belonging scores, and documented intervention effectiveness.

Stage 4: Optimization—Strategic Integration

ESG Profile: Predictive belonging analytics inform talent strategy, risk management, and strategic planning. Belonging infrastructure enables rather than follows business strategy.

Auditor Perspective: Sees sophisticated human capital risk management and strategic workforce optimization. Belonging infrastructure provides competitive advantage rather than just compliance capability.

Typical ESG Content: Strategic workforce planning based on belonging data, competitive talent attraction advantages, innovation pipeline acceleration through belonging optimization, and risk mitigation value quantification.

Stage 5: Continuous Innovation—Market Leadership

ESG Profile: Belonging data published in ESG reports and investor briefings. Organization becomes case study for human capital optimization. Belonging infrastructure creates measurable market advantages.

Auditor Perspective: Views organization as exemplar of social responsibility. Belonging infrastructure provides both ESG leadership and operational competitive advantage.

Typical ESG Content: Published belonging methodology, industry benchmark leadership, competitive advantages through workforce optimization, and replicable best practices for market leadership.

ESG Reporting Readiness Assessment

Organizations can assess their ESG readiness by evaluating their current belonging maturity:

- Can you predict retention six months in advance? (Stages 3+)
- Do belonging metrics appear in board reports? (Stages 3+)
- Can you trace ESG claims to operational processes? (Stages 3+)

- Do investors ask about your belonging infrastructure? (Stages 4+)
- Do competitors benchmark against your practices? (Stage 5)

The progression from crisis response to market leadership provides a clear development pathway for organizations seeking credible ESG positioning. Without belonging infrastructure, ESG claims remain vulnerable to credibility challenges that can create significant reputational and financial risk.

Integration Points with Existing Systems

Belonging succeeds when it integrates with systems leaders already manage rather than creating parallel processes. Organizations that embed belonging into existing business infrastructure see faster adoption and more sustainable results.

- **Talent Acquisition:** Embedding belonging criteria in job descriptions, redesigning interview processes to assess belonging competencies alongside technical skills, and training hiring managers to evaluate psychological safety and inclusion behaviors during candidate interactions.
- **Performance Management:** Including belonging behaviors in performance expectations and leadership competency models, making belonging competency a requirement for advancement to management roles, and incorporating team belonging scores into manager performance evaluations.
- **Strategic Planning:** Considering belonging impact in resource allocation decisions and organizational design

changes. Before major initiatives, leaders assess how proposed changes will affect belonging conditions and build mitigation strategies accordingly.
- **Risk Management:** Using belonging metrics as early indicators for retention risk in critical roles, compliance risk through psychological safety monitoring, and operational risk through collaboration tracking. Belonging data provides three-to-six-month advance warning of potential workforce disruptions.

Quarterly Business Review Integration

Advanced organizations include belonging metrics in the same meetings where they review revenue, margins, and operational KPIs:

- Belonging composite scores appear on standard executive dashboards.
- Department-level heat maps identify intervention priorities.
- Correlation tracking links belonging improvements to business outcomes.
- Resource allocation decisions factor belonging infrastructure needs.

Strategic Decision Integration

Mature belonging infrastructure informs major business choices by providing predictive intelligence about organizational readiness and human capital capacity.

Chapter 10: Making Social Impact Auditable—ESG and Belonging Infrastructure

- *Reorganizations:* Assess belonging impact before restructuring teams, identifying units with strong Connection and Support scores that can handle change more effectively. Teams with weak belonging foundations require additional change management resources and longer transition timelines.

- *Market Expansion:* Use belonging data to predict which units can handle growth pressure and increased collaboration requirements. Departments with high belonging scores demonstrate greater capacity for absorbing new team members and maintaining performance standards during expansion.

- *Technology Rollouts:* Plan change management based on current belonging conditions, with particular attention to Psychological Safety and Support scores. Units with strong belonging infrastructure adopt new technologies faster, while those with weak belonging require more intensive support resources.

- *Workforce Planning:* Factor belonging conditions into talent allocation decisions, succession planning, and capacity forecasting. High-belonging teams show more predictable retention patterns and higher internal mobility success rates.

- *Merger and Acquisition Planning:* Evaluate cultural compatibility through belonging assessments during due diligence, identifying integration risks before deal completion. Organizations with similar belonging profiles integrate more smoothly and preserve talent more effectively.

When belonging becomes a lens for improving existing systems rather than an additional system to manage, adoption accelerates and sustainability increases.

ESG credibility requires evidence that can withstand external scrutiny, but belonging infrastructure creates strategic value beyond regulatory compliance. It transforms one of the most expensive and unpredictable variables in business planning: human performance under different organizational conditions.

Most workforce planning treats people as constants when they're actually variables. The same person who underperforms in a low-belonging environment can become a top contributor when belonging conditions improve. Understanding this variable changes everything about how you forecast capacity, plan organizational growth, and model the true cost of strategic initiatives that depend on human coordination and collaboration.

CHAPTER 11

Why This Matters for Workforce Planning

Most workforce planning assumes people will perform consistently. But let's think about Alicia, whose experience reveals why that assumption fails. Alicia appeared in all the right workforce metrics. She had strong technical skills, met her deliverables, and showed up to meetings. Your standard workforce planning model would classify her as "retained talent"—not a flight risk, not requiring replacement budget.

But Alicia was mentally checking out. Her ideas got overlooked, her contributions went unrecognized, and she felt increasingly disconnected from her team. None of this showed up in traditional workforce metrics until the day she gave notice.

That's when the workforce planning assumptions collapsed. Alicia wasn't just another engineer—she was the person who caught critical bugs before they reached customers, the one who mentored junior developers, and the institutional memory for three major client integrations. Replacing her took eight months, cost $180,000 in recruitment and onboarding, and caused two project delays.

Your workforce planning models don't account for people like Alicia because they assume human performance is constant. It's not.

Most workforce planning relies on flawed assumptions. HR leaders assume 15 percent of engineers will quit this year, 30 percent of promotions will come from internal candidates, and each person produces X widgets per month. Then they add buffers for uncertainty and hope the math works out.

It doesn't work because workforce planning assumes people perform consistently. They don't. Belonging conditions primarily determine that variable.

I've worked with organizations where improvements reduced voluntary turnover. I've also seen breakdowns in belonging trigger talent exodus, derailing strategic initiatives. In both cases, the workforce planning assumptions became obsolete because the human performance equation had fundamentally changed.

Without belonging metrics, you're making workforce decisions based on incomplete information about what drives human performance.

The Variables You're Not Tracking

Traditional workforce planning focuses on tracking headcount, cost per hire, time to fill, and attrition rates. These metrics are helpful, but they show you only what has already occurred. You're missing the underlying conditions that drive those results.

What you're missing: People waste time figuring out what their boss actually wants, meetings take twice as long because

Chapter 11: Why This Matters for Workforce Planning

teams don't trust one another's motives, and employees focus on covering themselves instead of solving problems, and the innovation suppression from exclusionary practices. These invisible factors change your workforce model assumptions. When belonging conditions are weak, people underperform relative to their capability, leave sooner than economic models predict, and require more management oversight than budget assumptions include.

What you're missing: the cognitive load Alicia experienced from unclear expectations, the productivity drag from feeling excluded, and the innovation suppression when her technical insights were ignored. Traditional workforce planning doesn't track the invisible factors that determine whether someone like Alicia performs at capacity or goes through the motions.

When organizational resources fail to match job demands, performance declines and burnout increases.[249] Workforce planning that ignores this overestimates capacity and underestimates the risk of turnover.

When belonging conditions are strong, the opposite occurs: People perform closer to capacity, stay longer, and require less supervisory bandwidth. Your workforce becomes more productive per dollar and more predictable in performance.

The organizations with the most accurate workforce planning are the ones that factor belonging metrics into their human capital models.

---

249 Bakker & Demerouti, 2007.

Cultural Variables in Workforce Planning

Workforce planning must also account for cultural context variables that affect belonging implementation. In global organizations, the same belonging intervention may produce different retention and productivity outcomes across regions due to cultural differences in how safety, inclusion, and connection are interpreted and valued.

This creates planning complexity: Your belonging infrastructure may work differently in different markets, requiring location-specific calibration of belonging metrics and culturally adapted intervention strategies.

How Belonging Data Transforms Workforce Planning

Smart workforce leaders are discovering they can predict human performance problems months before they show up in traditional metrics.

Recent research shows belonging metrics can predict voluntary turnover six to eight months before standard indicators show risk, giving you time for proactive retention instead of scrambling to replace people.[250] Teams with strong belonging conditions need 23 percent less management oversight while delivering more consistent output, which changes your capacity planning assumptions entirely.[251]

---

[250] Quantum Workplace, *2025 HR Trends Report: Stop Reacting, Start Predicting* (2025), https://www.quantumworkplace.com/2025-workplace-trends-report.

[251] S. Patra, M. Pathan, M. Mahfouz, P. Zehtabi, W. Ouaja, D. Magazzeni, et al., "Capacity Planning and Scheduling for Jobs with Uncertainty in Resource Usage and Duration," *The Journal of Supercomputing* 80, no. 15 (2024): 22428–22461, https://doi.org/10.1007/s11227-024-06282-8.

Chapter 11: Why This Matters for Workforce Planning

Organizations using belonging-related data in workforce planning achieve 40 percent better accuracy in headcount forecasting and 28 percent lower recruiting costs through improved retention and internal mobility.[252] Instead of guessing based on historical patterns, you can model specific scenarios: What happens to productivity if Support scores drop five points? How does Connection strength affect cross-functional project success? What's the optimal belonging investment to hit target retention rates?

This transforms workforce planning from historical guesswork to predictive strategy. When belonging infrastructure provides predictable human performance variables, workforce planning becomes a competitive advantage rather than a defensive necessity.

How Belonging Changes Your Planning Numbers

Belonging conditions change your core planning assumptions:

Turnover Forecasting

- **Low belonging:** Elevated buffers needed, unpredictable exits concentrated in top performers, defensive hiring volume.
- **High belonging:** Stable projections, known risk tiers, strategic hiring instead of reactive replacement.

---

[252] Visier, *Workforce Intelligence Report: The Cost of Turnover* (Visier Analytics, 2023).

Internal Mobility

- **Low belonging:** Limited by trust gaps and unclear pathways, most growth filled externally, political navigation required.
- **High belonging:** Higher participation in stretch roles and mentorship, more positions filled internally, clearer development support.

Manager Capacity

- **Low belonging:** Time absorbed by re-recruitment and morale repair, reduced capacity for strategic work.
- **High belonging:** Time invested in development, coaching, and planning because reactive people management decreases.

Successor Pipeline

- **Low belonging:** Fragile due to disengagement and unclear pathways, external candidates needed for most roles.
- **High belonging:** Strengthened by clarity, connection, and support with robust internal pipeline.

Overall Efficiency

Workers held a rally outside the headquarters along with some allies and defense of what they view as a kind of rolling attack on both the science and the leadership of that organization.

Chapter 11: Why This Matters for Workforce Planning

- **Low belonging:** Inflation from rework, absenteeism, and redundancy requiring higher headcount for same output.
- **High belonging:** Leaner allocation with steadier output per employee and predictable capacity.

Your models predicted Alicia would stay because she had good compensation and met performance standards. But they missed that she scored low on Inclusion and Connection—predictive indicators that she was becoming a flight risk months before she started interviewing elsewhere.

Why AI Makes Belonging More Important, Not Less

There's a widespread assumption that automation will reduce the importance of human relationships at work. I've seen the opposite. As routine tasks become automated, the remaining human work becomes more collaborative, creative, and dependent on trust.

Automation eliminates routine work while increasing demand for collaborative problem-solving.[253] The jobs that survive require the interpersonal capabilities that belonging infrastructure enables.

As AI handles routine tasks, the work that remains requires collaboration, creativity, and institutional knowledge—exactly what people like Alicia provide when they're engaged. When they're not engaged, you lose the human capabilities that AI can't replace.

---

253 D. H. Autor, F. Levy, and R. J. Murnane, "The Skill Content of Recent Technological Change: An Empirical Exploration," *Quarterly Journal of Economics* 118, no. 4 (2003): 1279–1333, https://doi.org/10.1162/003355303322552801.

AI handles data processing, pattern recognition, and defined workflows effectively. What it can't handle is ambiguous problem-solving, cross-functional coordination, and adaptive response to novel situations. These capabilities require psychological safety to identify problems, inclusion to integrate diverse perspectives, and strong connection to enable rapid coordination.

Organizations that build belonging infrastructure now are preparing their human workforce to complement, rather than compete with, AI capabilities. Organizations that neglect their belonging infrastructure will find their human workforce operating below capacity, even as their technology investments increase.

The future workforce planning is directly tied to determining how people work most effectively with AI. Belonging infrastructure becomes the foundation for that optimization.

Belonging as Your Workforce Planning Advantage

Once you understand how belonging affects the fundamental variables in workforce planning, the next step is to treat it as a planning factor, not just a result. I've worked with CHROs and workforce planning teams that have made this shift, and I have seen dramatic improvements in forecast accuracy and operational efficiency.

Belonging changes three key planning assumptions:

- **Belonging makes performance more predictable:** When you have predictable retention patterns, faster onboarding and integration, and reduced defect rework, your

Chapter 11: Why This Matters for Workforce Planning

capacity planning becomes more accurate and your resource allocation more efficient.

- **Belonging protects against latent risk:** Earlier escalation of problems and steadier retention in compliance- and client-sensitive roles reduce the hidden costs that throw off workforce budgets.
- **Belonging enables execution:** More cross-team projects actually get finished, shorter time-to-decision cycles, and more reliable throughput mean your strategic initiatives deliver on time and on budget.

For executives, this translates directly into less uncertainty, more accurate forecasts, and greater value per employee. Instead of planning around human performance volatility, you're planning around human performance optimization.

Industry-Specific Workforce Variables

Workforce planning must account for industry-specific factors that affect belonging implementation and outcomes:

- **Regulatory Industries (healthcare, finance):** Compliance requirements may constrain certain belonging practices while making others (like psychological safety for error reporting) business critical.
- **Project-Based Industries (consulting, construction):** Belonging infrastructure must accommodate team formation and dissolution cycles.
- **Shift-Work Industries (manufacturing, retail):** Connection and Support systems require adaptation for multiple schedules and physical locations.

- **Remote-First Industries (technology, media):** All five pillars need digital-native implementation strategies.

Your belonging infrastructure investment and expected returns will vary based on these industry-specific dynamics.

Competitive Talent Dynamics

Workforce planning must account for competitive dynamics as more organizations invest in belonging infrastructure. The competitive advantage of belonging is not permanent—it requires continuous innovation and authentic implementation to maintain differentiation.

Three competitive scenarios to plan for:

- **Market Leadership:** Early belonging investment creates sustainable advantages in talent attraction and retention while competitors catch up.
- **Competitive Parity:** As belonging becomes widespread, advantages shift to operational excellence and authentic culture integration rather than just having belonging programs.
- **Laggard Risk:** Organizations that delay belonging investment face increasing talent disadvantages as workforce expectations evolve and high-quality candidates have more belonging-forward options.

The strategic workforce question becomes: How do we maintain belonging-based competitive advantages as the market evolves?

Chapter 11: Why This Matters for Workforce Planning

Long-Term Workforce Capability Building
Longitudinal workforce planning must account for how belonging infrastructure builds organizational capability:

- **Year 1-2:** Stabilized retention and improved productivity.
- **Year 3-4:** Enhanced internal mobility and leadership pipeline development.
- **Year 5+:** Sustainable competitive advantages in talent attraction and organizational resilience.

The workforce planning advantage of belonging infrastructure increases as the gap widens between organizations.

Five Ways Belonging Changes Planning
Belonging becomes a workforce lever when you embed it into five specific planning processes:

1 Attrition and Vacancy Management
Stop using flat percentage assumptions for turnover across all roles and functions. Instead, track predictable risk tiers by function and level, then tie your hiring buffers to those tiers. Don't use the same attrition assumptions for a high-belonging engineering team and a low-belonging sales team.

Track these costs in detail: Vacancy days translate to lost capacity, and avoidable exits translate to replacement costs. When you can quantify the buffer value, you can make better resource allocation decisions.

2 Mobility and Pipeline Development
Set internal slate ratio targets for roles above a certain level and

monitor stretch-role participation and mentorship uptake as leading indicators of internal pipeline health. Unlike the team that failed to register Alicia's contributions, high-belonging environments generate more internal candidates because people trust that development opportunities are genuine.

When people see credible advancement paths, they invest more in skill development and organizational commitment.[254] Internal mobility becomes self-reinforcing when trust infrastructure supports it.

Use the successor coverage ratio: Count how many people can step into each critical role within six months. Don't restructure or expand until you have belonging-supported succession coverage in place.

3 Ramp and Readiness Optimization

Define time-to-readiness curves by role family and link Support pillar indicators—such as tool access, training completion, and coaching cadence—to ramp up performance. When the Support infrastructure is strong, people reach full productivity faster.

Track cross-training completion and shadowing hours as precursors to internal redeployments. High-belonging environments facilitate internal mobility by encouraging people to support colleagues in transitioning into new roles.

4 Manager Capacity Liberation

This is one of the most significant hidden benefits I see. Track how much time managers spend recruiting, interviewing, and onboarding versus coaching their current team. Target

---

254 R. M. Kanter, *Men and Women of the Corporation* (Basic Books, 1977).

Chapter 11: Why This Matters for Workforce Planning

reductions in replacement-task load as a direct outcome of belonging stabilization.

When managers aren't constantly recruiting, onboarding, and managing morale crises, they can focus on capability building, strategic work, and team development. That manager capacity upgrade multiplies across your entire leadership pipeline.

5 Productivity Baselines

In low-belonging environments, productivity is suppressed by cognitive overhead from self-protection, coordination friction from low trust, and innovation constraint from risk aversion. In high-belonging environments, productivity approaches individual and team capacity because cognitive resources are directed toward contribution rather than protection. These aren't marginal differences. In my work, belonging improvements change workforce economics by 15–25 percent when measured comprehensively across retention, productivity, and management capacity.

Planning for the Long Term

When belonging operates as workforce infrastructure, your planning shifts from a defensive to a strategic approach. Instead of building buffers for unpredictable human volatility, you're optimizing systems for predictable human performance.

This extends your planning horizon because you can count on stability and capability development rather than hoping turnover doesn't spike during critical periods.

High-belonging organizations can make longer-term

workforce commitments because they have confidence in retention and development outcomes.

For workforce leaders building next year's plan, belonging metrics should inform your core assumptions about attrition rates, internal mobility success, ramp timelines, and management capacity. When those assumptions are grounded in belonging infrastructure rather than historical averages, your forecasts become strategic tools rather than educated guesses.

The Metrics That Actually Drive Planning Decisions

This measurement approach works with workforce planning teams to make belonging actionable rather than aspirational:

Leading Indicators—What You Can Control

You can influence these conditions through management action and resource allocation:

- **Belonging pillar metrics** include Psychological Safety index, Inclusion voice equity, Support access score, Connection density signals, and Purpose clarity. These tell you whether the foundation conditions are strengthening or weakening.
- **Development and mobility signals** include stretch-role acceptance rate, mentorship participation, internal slate depth, and manager one-on-one completion rates. These predict whether your internal pipeline will deliver when you need it.

Chapter 11: Why This Matters for Workforce Planning

Lagging Indicators—What You Can Predict

The most sophisticated organizations are moving beyond reactive workforce management to predictive capability. Instead of waiting for people to quit, they can see retention risks months before they materialize.

Belonging data predicts voluntary turnover eight to twelve weeks earlier than traditional exit patterns, giving you time for targeted retention efforts instead of scrambling for replacements.[255] Organizations tracking these patterns achieve 34 percent better accuracy in workforce planning and reduce hiring costs by 28 percent through improved retention and internal mobility forecasting.[256]

This shift from reactive to predictive workforce management represents a fundamental competitive advantage in talent-intensive industries.

- **Turnover and capacity metrics** include voluntary attrition by risk tier, vacancy days, time to fill, and time to readiness. These affect your hiring budgets and capacity planning.
- **Performance and risk indicators** include the successor coverage ratio, regrettable exit rate in critical roles, absenteeism percentage, and rework and defect rates. These impact your operational continuity and quality outcomes.

The key is to embed these in quarterly workforce reviews so belonging signals sit alongside headcount, cost, and output

---

255 Visier, 2023.
256 Quantum Workplace, 2025.

data. When belonging metrics appear in the same dashboard as traditional workforce metrics, leaders start managing them with the same discipline.

Planning Scenarios That Work

Stabilizing Attrition Risk
When Tier 2 engineering attrition exceeds the plan by two points, trigger Safety and Support interventions immediately, then convert 15–25 percent of next-quarter openings to internal redeployments instead of external hires. Adjust your hiring buffers down once vacancy days decline for two consecutive quarters.

This approach treats attrition as a systemic signal rather than individual departures, and uses internal mobility to stabilize capacity while belonging interventions take effect.

Lifting Internal Mobility
Where Inclusion voice equity is low and the internal slate ratio drops below 50 percent, consider running listening sessions combined with decision-ritual redesign. Set stretch-role targets per business unit and track mentorship-to-placement conversion rates.

This connects inclusion measurement to pipeline development, providing concrete actions that enhance both belonging conditions and internal talent supply.

Chapter 11: Why This Matters for Workforce Planning

Protecting Critical Roles

When successor coverage drops below 1.0 on any priority role, pause external backfills to prioritize cross-training and shadowing programs—tie manager bonus criteria to restored coverage of 1.5 or higher.

This ensures that belonging infrastructure supports succession planning rather than leaving critical roles vulnerable to single points of failure.

Why This Makes Planning More Strategic

Belonging makes planning more predictable by reducing workforce volatility on which your models rely.

As AI reduces or reshapes some roles, belonging becomes more valuable for the roles that remain. If you choose to hire a human, you must also choose to provide the infrastructure—Psychological Safety, Inclusion, Support, Connection, Purpose—that lets that hire outperform.

Without belonging infrastructure, forecasts revert to guesswork, buffers expand to accommodate volatility, and execution slows because human coordination becomes unreliable. With belonging infrastructure, workforce planning becomes a strategic capability rather than a defensive necessity.

Strategic Workforce Scenarios

Strong belonging infrastructure enables workforce strategies that aren't viable in low-trust environments:

- **Leaner management ratios** are lower because teams require less oversight and conflict mediation.
- **Higher internal promotion rates** occur because

development relationships and performance visibility improve.
- **Faster onboarding and integration** are facilitated by existing employees actively supporting new hires.
- **More ambitious cross-functional initiatives** are possible because coordination costs are lower.
- **Greater workforce flexibility** occurs because people adapt more easily to role changes and new team configurations.

These strategic options change the math on investments in automation, outsourcing, organizational design, and talent development.

Belonging as Workforce Insurance

One way to think about belonging infrastructure is as insurance against workforce volatility. Organizations with strong belonging can weather economic uncertainty, competitive talent pressure, and strategic change without catastrophic talent loss.

During the pandemic, I monitored how various organizations maintained their performance under stress. Those with a high level of belonging infrastructure before 2020 sustained productivity and morale better than those who attempted to build culture during the crisis.

Jane Dutton and Emily Heaphy's work on high-quality connections predicted this outcome: organizations with strong relationship infrastructure maintain resilience during crises, while those without it experience rapid capability degradation.[257] You can't build social capital when you need it most.

---

[257] Dutton & Heaphy, 2003.

The same pattern holds for other disruptions, such as acquisitions, leadership changes, market shifts, or competitive pressure. Belonging infrastructure creates workforce resilience that traditional HR programs can't replicate quickly enough during a crisis.

Making This Operational for Workforce Leaders

If you're responsible for workforce planning, belonging metrics should become part of your core planning tool kit, not a separate HR consideration.

Start by tracking pillar scores quarterly alongside traditional HR metrics to identify leading indicators of workforce risk. Too many workforce leaders are surprised by retention spikes that belonging data would have predicted months earlier.

Your workforce planning needs to catch patterns like Alicia's before you lose technical talent whose contributions you're only beginning to understand. Track belonging scores alongside performance metrics. Segment by role family and location. Model belonging improvements into retention forecasts. The goal is to enhance workforce planning metrics with predictive data about human performance conditions.

Segment workforce data by role family and location to identify areas with the highest likelihood of workforce volatility. A decline in your sales organization's support pillar signals different workforce risks than a Connection drop in engineering. Your hiring buffers and succession planning should reflect these differences.

Show CFOs the math: If belonging reduces turnover by 8 percent, here's how much money that saves in recruitment costs. When you can demonstrate to CFOs that belonging improvements reduce replacement costs by X percent and increase productivity by Y percent, you transition from a cost center to a value driver.

Use belonging trajectory as a factor in strategic workforce decisions such as expansion timing, reorganization sequencing, and automation priorities. Don't expand into new markets until you have the infrastructure to support rapid scaling. Don't reorganize until you understand how changes will affect the Connection and Support pillars.

I am not advocating that you replace traditional workforce metrics—rather, to enhance them with predictive data about human performance conditions. Belonging metrics tell you not just what happened, but what's likely to happen next.

The Workforce Business Case That Works

For workforce leaders building business cases, I help them translate belonging improvements into language that finance teams understand and approve.

- **Reduced replacement costs** from lower voluntary turnover. This is the easiest ROI to calculate and often the most significant single impact. Model the difference between current attrition rates and belonging-improved rates, and multiply by the average replacement cost.
- **Decreased time-to-productivity** from better onboarding integration and support. When Support infrastructure is strong, new hires reach full productivity faster. Track ramp time improvements and calculate the capacity value.
- **Lower management overhead** from reduced conflict resolution and morale maintenance. This is often the

Chapter 11: Why This Matters for Workforce Planning

hidden ROI that surprises executives. When managers aren't constantly fixing people's problems, they can focus on capability building and strategic work.

- **Higher internal promotion success rates** from better development relationships and clearer pathways. Internal promotions are less costly and ramp up faster than external hires. Track the improvement in the ratio and calculate the recruitment savings.

When modeled across a complete workforce, these improvements often justify belonging infrastructure investment within twelve to eighteen months. The math works, but you have to do the math.

Mark Huselid's research on high-performance work systems reveals similar ROI patterns: Investments in human capital infrastructure yield measurable returns through enhanced employee retention and productivity.[258]

Building Tomorrow's Workforce Advantage Today

The organizations that will have the most strategic workforce options are those building belonging infrastructure now, before they need it for a competitive advantage.

They'll be able to attract better talent because their employer brand reflects genuine belonging rather than aspirational messaging. They'll develop people faster because trust infrastructure accelerates learning and risk-taking. They'll retain high

---

258 M. A. Huselid, "The Impact of Human Resource Management Practices on Turnover, Productivity, and Corporate Financial Performance," *Academy of Management Journal* 38, no. 3 (1995): 635–672, https://doi.org/10.5465/256741.

performers longer because those people have reasons to stay beyond compensation.

What matters is that they'll be able to optimize human performance in whatever work environment emerges—whether that's hybrid, fully distributed, AI augmented, or configurations we haven't imagined yet.

Belonging infrastructure can improve current workforce outcomes; however, the long-term objective is in building the human capability foundation that enables future workforce strategy regardless of how technology and market conditions evolve.

The organizations that figure out human-AI collaboration, adapt quickly to market disruptions, and scale successfully into new geographies—they'll be the ones with belonging infrastructure that allows their human workforce to perform at capacity.

Once you determine to invest in belonging, make that investment strategically as part of workforce planning or reactively when workforce problems force your hand. One approach builds the one part nobody else gets right. The other manages a crisis.

We've covered the why, the what, the how, and the strategic applications. You now have everything you need to turn belonging from aspiration into organizational infrastructure. The only remaining question is whether you'll commit to action or continue managing belonging reactively.

Why This Matters for Workforce Planning

Most workforce planning assumes people will perform consistently when they actually don't, and belonging conditions determine the difference. When belonging is weak, people underperform compared to their capabilities, quit sooner than

Chapter 11: Why This Matters for Workforce Planning

expected, and require more management time than you budget for. When belonging is strong, people work closer to their potential, stay longer, and need less hand-holding. Your planning models overlook the hidden costs: mental energy wasted on unclear expectations, extra coordination time due to low trust, and lost productivity as people protect themselves. As AI takes over routine work, the jobs that remain need collaboration, creativity, and coordination—exactly what people can't do when belonging is broken.

ESG credibility requires evidence that can withstand external scrutiny, but belonging infrastructure creates strategic value beyond regulatory compliance. It transforms one of the most expensive and unpredictable variables in business planning: human performance under different organizational conditions.

Most workforce planning treats people as constants when they're actually variables. The same person who underperforms in a low-belonging environment can become a top contributor when belonging improves. Understanding this variable changes everything about how you forecast capacity, plan organizational growth, and model the true cost of strategic initiatives that depend on human coordination and collaboration.

CHAPTER 12

Your Next Steps

You now understand why belonging matters strategically, how it functions as measurable infrastructure, what the progression pathway looks like, and how to implement it.

Frameworks are useless without execution.

Most executives already believe belonging matters. If you made it this far, I would imagine it matters to you as well. The issue is whether you'll track and improve it like you do sales numbers or customer satisfaction scores.

The Decision Point

Every organization I work with reaches the same decision point: continue treating belonging as a cultural aspiration or start managing it as foundational infrastructure.

In today's talent market, workforce expectations are changing and scrutiny of culture is increasing. Belonging conditions either improve systematically or deteriorate gradually.

Organizations that invest in belonging now will have an advantage when talent competition intensifies. Those who wait will try to build culture during a crisis, which is more expensive and less effective.

Three Paths Forward

Three paths can be taken to move forward with belonging as infrastructure. The right path depends on your current maturity stage, organizational readiness, and the availability of resources.

Option 1: Do It Yourself

This works best if you have experienced project managers and leaders who will stay committed when things get difficult.

You start by conducting an honest organizational assessment using the mini-audit in Chapter 6, then identify your highest-leverage pillar opportunities based on current gaps and business impact potential.

Spend the first month getting leadership buy-in and measuring your starting point, manager enablement and metric integration in month two, and pilot expansion and process embedding in month three.

You'll need someone managing timelines, executives checking progress weekly, and the flexibility to change tactics when your data shows problems. You get organizational ownership and customization. You risk losing momentum when priorities shift or when implementation challenges arise without external expertise.

Chapter 12: Your Next Steps

Option 2: Get Help

This is suitable for organizations seeking improvement in belonging, supported by expert guidance and validated tools.

Start with a comprehensive assessment that measures all five belonging areas, segmented by role level, department, and relevant demographic dimensions. This data shows you where to focus first and helps you calculate the potential ROI.

Implementation includes training for executives, managers, and teams, as well as customized improvement plans tailored to your maturity stage and pillar profile. This is plus quarterly check-ins and adjustments based on what you learn, along with governance structures that sustain progress through leadership changes or operational pressures.

Guided implementation accelerates progress by leveraging proven methodologies and avoiding common pitfalls during implementation. The trade-off is higher cost and dependency on external expertise.

Option 3: Prepare First

This approach is particularly suitable for Stage 1 organizations or those undergoing significant leadership transitions, budget constraints, or competing strategic priorities.

You focus on building internal literacy about belonging as business infrastructure, establishing a measurement baseline through periodic pulse surveys, identifying potential pilot opportunities and internal champions, and preparing business cases for the future where systems are held together by process, not personalities.

The preparation phase creates organizational readiness for belonging work when conditions improve. The risk is that preparation becomes procrastination while belonging conditions deteriorate.

The quick reference cards in Appendix E provide audience-specific reading guides and a seven-day kickoff timeline.

What Success Looks Like

Regardless of which direction you choose, successful belonging implementation produces predictable outcomes:

- Retention improvements that reduce replacement costs and preserve institutional knowledge. Teams work together more smoothly and people go beyond their basic job requirements. Innovation accelerates when diverse perspectives shape decision-making. Earlier problem detection and open communication reduce risk. Higher trust enables strategic agility and faster adaptation to change.
- ROI timelines depend on the organizational maturity and the scope of the intervention. Early-stage organizations typically require twelve to eighteen months to achieve a measurable impact, while mature organizations normally see gains within six to nine months. Setting unrealistic timeline expectations undermines executive commitment when work that requires sustained investment is involved.

Resource Requirements

Belonging infrastructure requires ongoing investment directly aligned with other strategic advantages. This typically costs between 0.5 percent and 1.5 percent of your total payroll—mostly for training and measurement tools. Under-resource this and it will fail regardless of executive commitment or the quality of the framework.

For self-directed implementation, the primary investment is leadership time and internal project management capacity. Most organizations allocate 10 percent to 15 percent of one senior leader's time plus supporting HR and analytics resources.

For guided implementation, the investment includes external partnership costs, typically ranging from $50,000 to $250,000 annually, depending on organizational size and scope, plus similar internal time allocation for change management and execution.

Reduced turnover alone typically exceeds implementation investment within twelve to eighteen months for most organizations.

Implementation Realities: Beyond Common Pitfalls

Successful belonging implementation requires understanding not just what works, but what fails and why. Research reveals four critical factors often overlooked:

- **Failure Factor 1—Structural Conflicts:** Belonging initiatives fail when they conflict with existing institutional structures, regardless of leadership commitment or resource allocation.
- **Failure Factor 2—Cultural Misalignment:** Universal frameworks require local adaptation. What works in one cultural context may be counterproductive in another.
- **Failure Factor 3—Ethical Blind Spots:** Organizations that implement belonging measurement without addressing

privacy, transparency, and consent concerns often find that measurement itself undermines trust.
- **Failure Factor 4—Competitive Assumptions:** As belonging becomes widespread, maintaining competitive advantage requires authentic integration rather than program implementation.

Understanding these factors transforms belonging from a hopeful initiative into a strategic capability that can withstand the complexities of real organizational life.

Organizations that avoid these pitfalls see sustained improvements in belonging. Organizations that experience initiative fatigue tend to revert to previous patterns.

Implementation Reality

These concepts are straightforward in theory but complex in practice. Successful implementation requires approaches detailed in comprehensive frameworks. Organizations that attempt to scale belonging using only a basic understanding consistently encounter implementation problems that comprehensive methodologies help avoid.

The Urgency Factor

While belonging work takes time, starting is urgent. Market conditions, workforce expectations, and competitive dynamics are shifting in ways that make belonging infrastructure increasingly essential.

Organizations that begin building belonging capability now will have a strategic advantage when external pressures increase.

Chapter 12: Your Next Steps

Organizations that wait will find themselves building culture during a crisis—always a more difficult and less effective process. The best time to build belonging infrastructure is before you need it to carry you through challenging periods.

Making the Commitment

Belonging change requires executive commitment beyond quarterly results. It requires viewing belonging as a long-term competitive advantage rather than short-term morale improvement.

The commitment includes allocating adequate resources, maintaining measurement discipline, protecting belonging initiatives during budget pressure, and modeling belonging behaviors consistently at the leadership level. Executive sponsorship requires actively modeling the right behaviors, not just allocating resources. Belonging scales through leadership demonstration, executives must consistently model vulnerability, inclusion, and support in their daily interactions. Delegation without modeling creates cynicism that undermines building something that actually works on a sustained basis.

Without this commitment, belonging initiatives become performative rather than transformative. With it, belonging becomes a sustainable edge.

Organizations either measure belonging like revenue or they manage belonging crises. Appendixes C, D, and E provide the financial models, maturity road maps, and governance structures that turn the framework into a competitive advantage.

Your Decision Today

You now have the frameworks, measurement tools, implementation plans, and business case for treating belonging as organizational infrastructure. What matters now is your organization's commitment to action.

Belonging matters—the evidence is overwhelming. What matters is whether you'll measure and manage it with the same rigor you apply to other systems critical to performance.

The organizations that answer "yes" gain a human capital advantage that compounds over time. Those who answer "maybe" or "later" tend to manage belonging crises reactively, rather than proactively building capability.

The choice is yours, and waiting makes it harder.

Taking Action This Week

If you're ready to move from understanding to implementation, take these steps this week:

Complete the mini-audit with your leadership team and discuss the results honestly. Identify your organization's current maturity stage and prioritize the areas of your weakest pillars.

Decide which implementation path aligns with your organizational readiness and resource availability. Calendar the first thirty days of foundation work, regardless of which path you choose.

Begin building internal alignment by sharing this field guide with key stakeholders and scheduling a discussion on belonging as an agenda item in your next executive team meeting.

Shift your language from "we should do this" to "we will do this" and establish the measurement and accountability structures that make belonging improvement inevitable rather than aspirational.

Chapter 12: Your Next Steps

The difference between organizations that transform their belonging infrastructure and those that don't isn't commitment to the idea—it's commitment to the discipline of improvement. Your next ninety days will determine whether belonging becomes an operational advantage or remains a cultural aspiration. Will your belonging infrastructure save Alicia?

Your Next Steps

Understanding frameworks doesn't change organizations—doing something does. You have three choices: do it yourself if you have strong project management skills and committed leaders, get expert help if you want proven methods and guidance, or spend time preparing if you're not yet ready. Whatever you choose, belonging costs money like any other business system—usually 0.5 percent to 1.5 percent of payroll per year, but you typically get that back within twelve to eighteen months from people quitting less. Organizations that foster a sense of belonging now will have an advantage when talent competition intensifies. Those who wait will try to build culture during a crisis, which is more expensive and less effective.

The organizations that build belonging infrastructure in the next eighteen months will have a decisive advantage when the next economic disruption hits. They'll retain talent while competitors scramble to replace people. They'll execute strategy while others get bogged down in coordination overhead. They'll adapt to market changes while others fragment under pressure.

You have the frameworks, the evidence, and the implementation methodology. The only question left is whether you'll take responsibility for building it.

CLOSING THOUGHTS

Why Belonging Is Your Responsibility

I want to end where we started, with the recognition that belonging is infrastructure, and infrastructure is always someone's responsibility.

If you're reading this, you're likely in a position to influence how your organization operates. You make decisions about resource allocation, strategic priorities, and system design. You decide which metrics get tracked in quarterly reviews and which problems get budget to fix them.

That means belonging is your responsibility.

The Moral Case

People spend the majority of their waking hours at work. For most adults, workplace relationships constitute their primary social network. The conditions you create at work don't just affect productivity—they affect human well-being.

When those conditions consistently signal that someone doesn't belong, the impact extends far beyond quarterly performance metrics. It affects confidence, mental health, family relationships, and life trajectory. When talented people quit because they felt excluded or undervalued, you've wasted human potential.

Conversely, when workplace conditions enable people to contribute authentically, develop new skills and build authentic relationship, the positive impact compounds through families, communities, and the next generation.

You have the power to create conditions where human beings flourish or merely survive. That's not a small responsibility.

The Business Necessity

Beyond the human impact, there's a business reality. Belonging infrastructure enables organizations to build a sustainable competitive advantage through enhanced human capability.

Virtually all organizations face the same fundamental challenge: executing strategy through people. Strategy doesn't implement itself. Innovation doesn't happen in isolation. Customer experience doesn't improve solely through process optimization.

All organizational outcomes depend on people being willing and able to contribute their best thinking, highest effort, and most creative problem-solving. Belonging conditions directly influence both.

Companies that invest in belonging infrastructure see higher retention, faster innovation, and better financial results. They attract better talent, retain high performers for longer, execute strategy more efficiently, adapt to change more effectively, and recover from setbacks more quickly.

Closing: Why Belonging Is Your Responsibility

Huselid's landmark research on high-performance work systems demonstrated this connection: Organizations that invest in human capital infrastructure experience measurable returns in productivity, retention, and financial performance.[259] These fundamental differences in organizational capability compound over time, ultimately influencing market position, financial performance, and strategic optionality.

Belonging infrastructure is business infrastructure. Ignoring it costs you competitive advantage.

The Leadership Test

You can determine whether leaders understand their responsibility for belonging by asking them what they measure, what resources they allocate, and how they hold people accountable for belonging outcomes.

Leaders who understand belonging as infrastructure measure it, invest in it consistently, and integrate it into performance expectations. Leaders who treat belonging as a cultural aspiration mention it in speeches but don't track it in dashboards.

Most leaders care about workplace culture, but caring isn't enough without action. Infrastructure requires design, measurement, and maintenance.

Look at your calendar right now. When did you last review belonging data? If it's been more than a month, you're telling your organization that belonging doesn't matter. Change that today. How much you spend on belonging tells people whether you actually care about it or just talk about it. Your

---

[259] Huselid, 1995.

accountability structures for belonging behaviors tell managers and employees what matters for advancement.

These become tests of leadership integrity, not just management skill.

The Systems Thinking Requirement

You can't build belonging through individual gestures. It requires changes to how decisions get made, meetings take place, resources get allocated, how employees are enabled, and people get recognized and rewarded.

Belonging fails when you delegate it to HR while expecting business results. It fails when you give inspiring speeches but don't change how meetings run, decisions get made, or people get promoted. It fails when you communicate values but ignore the daily systems that contradict them.

Schein's research on organizational culture demonstrates why culture is shaped by what leaders pay attention to, measure, and reward, rather than by what they say in speeches.[260] Systems shape behavior more powerfully than good intentions.

Belonging requires the same systems discipline you apply to financial management, operational efficiency, or customer experience. It requires understanding interdependencies, measuring leading indicators, and designing feedback loops that enable continuous improvement.

Most important, it requires recognizing that belonging infrastructure is executive infrastructure. It's part of the foundational systems that determine whether your organization can realize its full potential.

---

260 Schein, 1985.

Closing: Why Belonging Is Your Responsibility

The Intergenerational Perspective

The workforce you're building, which serves as belonging infrastructure for today, benefits your current employees as well as the talent pipeline that will determine your organizational capability for the next decade.

Younger workforce generations expect belonging as a baseline condition. They've grown up with greater exposure to diverse perspectives, higher expectations for authentic inclusion, and less tolerance for organizational cultures that require identity suppression or defensive navigation.

Jean Twenge's generational research documents these shifting expectations—younger workers prioritize psychological safety and authentic inclusion as nonnegotiable workplace conditions.[261] Your next hire is evaluating whether your culture is worth joining. Your best employees are deciding whether it's worth staying. Every day you delay building belonging infrastructure, you're choosing talent loss over talent retention.

Organizations that build belonging infrastructure now will have access to the whole talent market. Organizations that don't will only attract people desperate enough to tolerate bad workplace cultures.

The goal is staying competitive for talent, not accommodating generational preferences.

The Ripple Effect

Organizations with a strong sense of belonging become talent magnets. People want to work there, customers want to engage with them, and partners want to collaborate with them.

---

261 J. M. Twenge, *Generation Me: Why Today's Young Americans Are More Confident, Assertive, Entitled—and More Miserable than Ever Before* (Atria, 2010).

The internal conditions you create become external brand differentiators.

Employees from high-belonging organizations carry those behavioral patterns into their communities, families, and future roles. They become ambassadors for what workplace culture can be at its best.

Organizations with weak belonging infrastructure create the opposite ripple effect. Talent leaves, reputation suffers, and people carry negative workplace experiences into other contexts.

You're not just designing internal systems—you're contributing to broader patterns about how humans treat each other in professional settings.

The Legacy Question

This comes down to legacy. Not a personal legacy, but an organizational legacy and a societal legacy.

You're either building systems where people like Alicia get heard, or you're building systems where they adapt themselves to survive. Your measurement and spending decisions determine which one you get.

Or will you build systems where people must adapt to survive? Where groupthink passes for alignment? Where support depends on politics and relationships feel transactional?

The choice is made daily through measurement priorities, resource allocation decisions, accountability structures, and operational design choices.

Your Commitment

If you're convinced that belonging infrastructure matters for both human and business reasons, then your responsibility is clear: Commit to building it.

Measure belonging as rigorously as financial performance. Spend money on it like you do on technology or marketing. Hold leaders accountable for results with the exact expectations you have for operational outcomes.

It means recognizing that belonging infrastructure is never finished—it requires continuous attention, periodic refresh, and ongoing protection against forces that erode trust, inclusion, and connection.

The Call to Action

You now have the frameworks, evidence, and implementation guidance to establish a belonging infrastructure within your organization. You understand why it matters strategically, how it works operationally, and what it requires systematically.

What matters now is your commitment to action.

Belonging improves when leaders decide it's important enough to measure, invest in, and protect over time. It improves when belonging infrastructure becomes as fundamental to organizational design as financial systems or operational processes.

Jim Collins and Jerry Porras found that lasting organizational excellence requires consistent attention to basic capabilities, not just financial metrics.[262] Belonging infrastructure follows the same principle—it requires intentional building and maintenance.

---

262 J. Collins and J. I. Porras, *Built to Last: Successful Habits of Visionary Companies* (Harper Business, 1994).

That decision—and that leadership—starts with you.

The people in your organization are waiting to see whether belonging will remain aspirational language or become an operational reality. Your customers are evaluating whether your values match your practices. Your future talent pipeline is watching how you treat the people you have now.

Belonging infrastructure will determine your organizational success—will you build it intentionally or let it develop accidentally?

Your choice shapes organizational character, which directly affects performance through human capability.

Jeffrey Pfeffer's research on competitive advantage through people validates this perspective—in knowledge-intensive industries, organizational character becomes a strategic asset because it determines how effectively human talent can be leveraged.[263] Character enables performance.

Belonging is infrastructure, and infrastructure is always someone's responsibility. If you're reading this, that responsibility is yours.

Make it count.

---

263 J. Pfeffer, *Competitive Advantage through People* (Harvard Business School Press, 1994).

Bibliography

Achievers Workforce Institute. *Belonging at Work Report*. Achievers, 2021.

———. *The Belonging Blueprint: How to Create a Culture of Belonging for Every Worker in Your Organization*. Achievers, 2025. https://www.achievers.com/resources/white-papers/workforce-institute-belonging-blueprint/.

Agency for Healthcare Research and Quality (AHRQ). *Annual Perspective: Psychological Safety for Healthcare Staff*. Agency for Healthcare Research and Quality, 2023.

Al-Twairesh, N., H. Al-Negheimish, and A. M. Al-Salman. "Surface and Deep Features Ensemble for Sentiment Analysis of Arabic Tweets." *IEEE Access* 11 (2023): 84122–84131. https://doi.org/10.1109/ACCESS.2023.3414097.

American Society for Microbiology. *ASM Ethics: Upholding Trust, Integrity, and Innovation in Science*. 2023. https://asm.org/asm-ethics.

Armenakis, A. A., and A. G. Bedeian. "Organizational Change: A Review of Theory and Research in the 1990s." *Journal of Management* 25, no. 3 (1999): 293–315. https://doi.org/10.1177/014920639902500303.

Autor, D. H., F. Levy, and R. J. Murnane. "The Skill Content of Recent Technological Change: An Empirical Exploration." *Quarterly Journal of Economics* 118, no. 4 (2003): 1279–1333. https://doi.org/10.1162/003355303322552801.

Bain & Company. *Resilience as a Competitive Advantage.* 2022. https://www.bain.com/insights.

———. *The Multiplier Effect of Belonging.* Bain & Company Insights, 2023. https://www.bain.com/insights/the-multiplier-effect-of-belonging/.

Bakker, A. B., and E. Demerouti. "The Job Demands–Resources Model: State of the Art." *Journal of Managerial Psychology* 22, no. 3 (2007): 309–328. https://doi.org/10.1108/02683940710733115.

Bakker, A. B., and E. Demerouti. "Job Demands-Resources Theory: Taking Stock and Looking Forward." *Journal of Occupational Health Psychology* 22, no. 3 (2017): 273–285.

Baumeister, R. F., and M. R. Leary. "The Need to Belong: Desire for Interpersonal Attachments as a Fundamental Human Motivation." *Psychological Bulletin* 117, no. 3 (1995): 497–529. https://doi.org/10.1037/0033-2909.117.3.497.

Berkeley Othering & Belonging Institute. *Belonging Design Principles.* University of California, Berkeley, 2023. https://belonging.berkeley.edu/belongingdesignprinciples.

Bibliography

BetterUp. *The Value of Belonging at Work: New Frontiers for Inclusion.* 2019. https://grow.betterup.com/resources/the-value-of-belonging-at-work-the-business-case-for-investing-in-workplace-inclusion.

———. *The Business Case for Belonging Infrastructure.* BetterUp Labs, 2024.

Bollen, K. A. *Structural Equations with Latent Variables.* New York: Wiley, 1989.

Boston Consulting Group (BCG). *Inclusion Isn't Just Nice. It's Necessary.* 2023. https://www.bcg.com/publications/2023/how-to-improve-inclusion-in-the-workplace.

———. "Leadership That Prioritizes Inclusion in the Workplace Can Slash Attrition Risk." February 21, 2023. https://www.bcg.com/press/22february2023-leadership-that-prioritizes-inclusion-can-slash-attrition-risk.

Bridge & Rhino. "Leading with the Brain in Mind: The Neuroscience of Trust and Collaboration." March 16, 2025. https://bridgeandrhino.com/articles/leading-with-the-brain-in-mind-the-neuroscience-of-trust-and-collaboration/.

Butler, T., E. Falk, and A. M. Kleinbaum. *Belonging in Organizational Networks: Integrating Psychological and Social Network Perspectives on Inclusion.* Working Paper, University of Pennsylvania & Dartmouth College, 2024. https://faculty.tuck.dartmouth.edu/images/uploads/faculty/adam-kleinbaum/Workplace_Inclusion.pdf.

Cacioppo, J. T., and L. C. Hawkley. "Perceived Social Isolation and Cognition." *Trends in Cognitive Sciences* 13, no. 10 (2009): 447–454. https://doi.org/10.1016/j.tics.2009.05.005.

Catalyst. "Catalyst Awards 2025: Advancing Gender Equity and Workplace Inclusion." Catalyst, March 11, 2025. https://www.catalyst.org/en-us/about/stories/2025/catalyst-awards-summary.

Christian, M. S., A. S. Garza, and J. E. Slaughter. "Work Engagement: A Quantitative Review and Test of Its Relations with Task and Contextual Performance." *Personnel Psychology* 64, no. 1 (2011): 89–136. https://doi.org/10.1111/j.1744-6570.2010.01203.x.

Clark, T. R. *The Four Stages of Psychological Safety: Defining the Path to Inclusion and Innovation.* Berrett-Koehler, 2020.

Collins, J., and J. I. Porras. *Built to Last: Successful Habits of Visionary Companies.* Harper Business, 1994.

Crisis Response Improvement Strategy (CRIS) Committee. *Recommendations for Behavioral Health Crisis Response in Washington.* Results Washington, 2019. https://results.wa.gov/.

David, T., and H. A. Shih. "Securing Success: Exploring Attachment Dynamics and Psychological Safety for Adaptive Behaviors in a Military Context." *Journal of Occupational and Organizational Psychology* 97, no. 2 (2024): 327–347. https://bpspsychub.onlinelibrary.wiley.com/doi/abs/10.1111/joop.12494.

Deloitte. *Does a Company's ESG Score Have a Measurable Impact on Its Market Value?* 2023. https://www.deloitte.com/ch/en/services/consulting-financial/research/does-a-company-esg-score-have-a-measurable-impact-on-its-market-value.html.

———. *Ethics and the Future of Human Capital Data.* Deloitte Center for Ethical Leadership, 2024.

———. *2025 Global Human Capital Trends: Turning Tensions into Triumphs*. Deloitte Insights, 2025. https://www2.deloitte.com/us/en/insights/topics/talent/human-capital-trends/2025.html.

Demerouti, E., A. B. Bakker, F. Nachreiner, and W. B. Schaufeli. "The Job Demands–Resources Model of Burnout." *Journal of Applied Psychology* 86, no. 3 (2001): 499–512. https://doi.org/10.1037/0021-9010.86.3.499.

DeVellis, R. F. *Scale Development: Theory and Applications*. 4th ed. Sage, 2017.

Diversio. *Understanding the DEI Maturity Model*. 2024. https://diversio.com/dei-maturity-model/.

Dixon-Fyle, S., K. Dolan, V. Hunt, and S. Prince. *Diversity Wins: How Inclusion Matters*. McKinsey & Company, 2020. https://www.mckinsey.com/featured-insights/diversity-and-inclusion/diversity-wins-how-inclusion-matters.

Dover, T. L., C. R. Kaiser, and B. Major. "Belonging Initiatives and Organizational Change: Patterns of Failure and Pathways for Success." *Journal of Management Studies* 60, no. 3 (2023): 717–743. https://doi.org/10.1111/joms.12907.

Dunson, C. C. *Sense of Belonging in the Workplace: Development and Validation of a Scale*. Doctoral dissertation, Liberty University, 2025. https://digitalcommons.liberty.edu/doctoral/7134/.

Dutton, J. E., and E. D. Heaphy. "The Power of High-Quality Connections." In *Positive Organizational Scholarship*, edited by K. S. Cameron, J. E. Dutton, and R. E. Quinn, 263–278. Berrett-Koehler, 2003.

Eberl, P., D. Geiger, and M. S. Aßländer. "Repairing Trust in an Organization after Integrity Violations: The Ambivalence of Organizational Rule Adjustments." *Organization Studies* 36, no. 9 (2015): 1205–1235. https://doi.org/10.1177/0170840615585335.

Edmondson, A. C. "Psychological Safety and Learning Behavior in Work Teams." *Administrative Science Quarterly* 44, no. 2 (1999): 350–383. https://doi.org/10.2307/2666999.

Edmondson, A. C., and Z. Lei. "Psychological Safety: The History, Renaissance, and Future of an Interpersonal Construct." *Annual Review of Organizational Psychology and Organizational Behavior* 1, no. 1 (2014): 23–43. https://doi.org/10.1146/annurev-orgpsych-031413-091305.

Eisenberger, N. I. "The Pain of Social Disconnection: Examining the Shared Neural Underpinnings of Physical and Social Pain." *Nature Reviews Neuroscience* 13 (2012): 421–434. https://doi.org/10.1038/nrn3231.

Eisenberger, N. I., and M. D. Lieberman. "Why Rejection Hurts: A Common Neural Alarm System for Physical and Social Pain." *Trends in Cognitive Sciences* 8, no. 7 (2004): 294–300. https://doi.org/10.1016/j.tics.2004.05.010.

Eisenberger, N. I., M. D. Lieberman, and K. D. Williams. "Does Rejection Hurt? An fMRI Study of Social Exclusion." *Science* 302, no. 5643 (2003): 290–292. https://doi.org/10.1126/science.1089134.

Ellis, S., and J. Yarker. "Speak-Up Cultures: Creating Psychological Safety." *Harvard Business Review*, 2019.

Bibliography

Federal Emergency Management Agency (FEMA). "Lesson 4: Building and Rebuilding Trust." In *Leadership and Influence (IS-240.b) Student Manual*, 4.1–4.24. FEMA Emergency Management Institute, 2019. https://training.fema.gov/emiweb/is/is240b/sm%20files/sm_04.pdf.

Festinger, L. "Informal Social Communication." *Psychological Review* 57, no. 5 (1950): 271–282. https://doi.org/10.1037/h0056932.

———. *A Theory of Cognitive Dissonance*. Stanford University Press, 1957.

Fixsen, D. L., Naoom, S. F., Blase, K. A., Friedman, R. M., & Wallace, F. (2005). *Implementation research: A synthesis of the literature*. University of South Florida.

Google re:Work. *Understand Team Effectiveness: Guide: Understand Team Effectiveness*. 2016. https://rework.withgoogle.com/intl/en/guides/understanding-team-effectiveness.

Gallup. *Employee Engagement and Performance Report*. Gallup, 2020.

Hagerty, B. M., and K. Patusky. "Developing a Measure of Sense of Belonging." *Nursing Research* 44, no. 1 (1995): 9–13. https://doi.org/10.1097/00006199-199501000-00003.

Harter, J. K., F. L. Schmidt, S. Agrawal, and S. K. Plowman. *Employee Engagement and Performance at Work*. Gallup, 2020.

HR&P Human Resources. "Replacing Employees Costs Big Dollars." *HR&P Human Resources Blog*, April 1, 2025. https://hrp.net/hrp-blog/replacing-employees-costs-big-dollars/.

Hurst, A. *The Purpose Economy*. Elevate, 2014.

Huselid, M. A. "The Impact of Human Resource Management Practices on Turnover, Productivity, and Corporate Financial Performance." *Academy of Management Journal* 38, no. 3 (1995): 635–672. https://doi.org/10.5465/256741.

Institute for Corporate Productivity (i4cp). *Priorities & Predictions Report.* 2024. https://go.i4cp.com/hubfs/Download%20Assets/2024%20Priorities%20and%20Predictions%20Report%20-%20i4cp.pdf.

———. *The Productivity Predicament: Executive Brief.* 2024. https://go.i4cp.com/hubfs/Download%20Assets/2024%20Priorities%20and%20Predictions%20Report%20-%20i4cp.pdf.

———. *Strategic HR: Priorities and Predictions for 2025.* 2025. https://www.i4cp.com/predictions.

———. *Workforce Collaboration & Team Performance Research.* 2025. https://www.i4cp.com/kc/leadership/collaboration.

Jaeger, L., S. Chen, and K. Morrison. "Longitudinal Analysis of Workplace Belonging and Organizational Outcomes." *Journal of Applied Psychology* 109, no. 4 (2024): 412–428.

Kahn, W. A. "Psychological Conditions of Personal Engagement and Disengagement at Work." *Academy of Management Journal* 33, no. 4 (1990): 692–724. https://doi.org/10.2307/256287.

Kanter, R. M. *Men and Women of the Corporation.* Basic Books, 1977.

Kaplan, R. S., and D. P. Norton. *The Balanced Scorecard: Translating Strategy into Action.* Harvard Business School Press, 1996.

Klein, K. J., and J. S. Sorra. "The Challenge of Innovation Implementation." *Academy of Management Review* 21, no. 4 (1996): 1055–1080. https://doi.org/10.5465/amr.1996.9704071863.

Kline, R. B. *Principles and Practice of Structural Equation Modeling.* 5th ed. New York: Guilford Press, 2023.

Knauf, E. "The Belonging Standard: A Framework for Thriving Organizations." *LinkedIn Articles*, December 10, 2024. https://www.linkedin.com/pulse/belonging-standard-framework-thriving-organizations-eric-knauf-8hawe.

Kotter, J. P. *Leading Change.* Harvard Business School Press, 1996.

Kramer, R. M., and R. J. Lewicki. "Trust Repair in Organizations: Twenty Years of Progress and Future Directions." *Annual Review of Organizational Psychology and Organizational Behavior* 8 (2021): 259–283. https://doi.org/10.1146/annurev-orgpsych-012420-083025.

Lee, D., J.-W. Gu, and H.-W. Jung. "Process Maturity Models: Classification by Application Sectors and Validities Studies." *Journal of Software: Evolution and Process* 31, no. 4 (2019): e2161. https://doi.org/10.1002/smr.2161.

Lee, S. Y., and H. A. Neville. "The Definition and Measurement of Sense of Belonging in Higher Education: A Systematic Review." *International Journal of Educational Research* 122 (2024): 102178. https://doi.org/10.1016/j.ijer.2024.102178.

Lieberman, M. D., and N. I. Eisenberger. "Pains and Pleasures of Social Life." *Science* 323, no. 5916 (2009): 890–891. https://doi.org/10.1126/science.1170008.

LinkedIn. *2023 Workplace Learning Report.* LinkedIn Learning, 2023.

Mallick, M. *Reimagine Inclusion: Debunking 13 Myths to Transform Your Workplace*. Wiley, 2023.

Maslow, A. H. "A Theory of Human Motivation." *Psychological Review* 50, no. 4 (1943): 370–396. https://doi.org/10.1037/h0054346.

May, D. R., R. L. Gilson, and L. M. Harter. "The Psychological Conditions of Meaningfulness, Safety, and Availability and the Engagement of the Human Spirit at Work." *Journal of Occupational and Organizational Psychology* 77, no. 1 (2004): 11–37. https://doi.org/10.1348/096317904322915892.

Mayer, R. C., J. H. Davis, and F. D. Schoorman. "An Integrative Model of Organizational Trust." *Academy of Management Review* 20, no. 3 (1995): 709–734. https://doi.org/10.5465/amr.1995.9508080335.

McKinsey & Company. *Organizational Resilience and Culture*. 2020. https://www.mckinsey.com/business-functions/organization/our-insights/organizational-resilience-and-culture.

Miranda-Wolff, A. *Cultures of Belonging: Building Inclusive Organizations That Last*. HarperCollins Leadership, 2022.

Netemeyer, R. G., J. G. Maxham, and D. R. Lichtenstein. "Store Manager Behaviors and Frontline Employee Performance." *Journal of Marketing Research* 40, no. 3 (2003): 271–286. https://doi.org/10.1509/jmkr.40.3.271.19236.

Newman, A., R. Donohue, and N. Eva. "Psychological Safety: A Systematic Review of the Literature." *Human Resource Management Review* 27, no. 3 (2017): 521–535.

Nishii, L. H. "The Benefits of Climate for Inclusion." *Academy of Management Journal* 56, no. 6 (2013): 1754–1774. https://doi.org/10.5465/amj.2009.0823.

Office of the U.S. Surgeon General. *Framework for Workplace Mental Health and Well-Being.* U.S. Department of Health & Human Services, 2022.

Palus, C., and T. McMullen. *Human Capital Measurement and Reporting: The New Imperative for HR and Investor Relations.* Center for Workforce Analytics, Northeastern University, 2023. https://cps.northeastern.edu/wp-content/uploads/2023/01/Human-Capital-Measurement-and-Reporting.pdf.

Patra, S., M. Pathan, M. Mahfouz, P. Zehtabi, W. Ouaja, D. Magazzeni, et al. "Capacity Planning and Scheduling for Jobs with Uncertainty in Resource Usage and Duration." *The Journal of Supercomputing* 80, no. 15 (2024): 22428–22461. https://doi.org/10.1007/s11227-024-06282-8.

Petersen, K. J. "Maturity Models in Organizational Change." *Journal of Business Strategy* 31, no. 4 (2010): 12–19.

Pfeffer, J. *Competitive Advantage through People.* Harvard Business School Press, 1994.

Prosci. *Global Insights about Organizational Change Today: Change Fatigue and Resistance.* 2024. https://www.prosci.com/blog/global-insights-about-organizational-change-today.

Pratt, M. G., and B. E. Ashforth. "Fostering Meaningfulness in Working and at Work." In *Positive Organizational Scholarship*, edited by K. S. Cameron, J. E. Dutton, and R. E. Quinn, 309–327. Berrett-Koehler, 2003.

Quantum Workplace. *2025 HR Trends Report: Stop Reacting, Start Predicting.* 2025. https://www.quantumworkplace.com/2025-workplace-trends-report.

Queensland Public Sector Commission. *Leadership Competencies for Queensland Framework.* Brisbane, Australia: Queensland Government, 2019. https://www.forgov.qld.gov.au/leadership-competencies-queensland

Raudenbush, S. W., and A. S. Bryk. *Hierarchical Linear Models: Applications and Data Analysis Methods.* 2nd ed. Sage, 2002.

Remington, T., A. Chen, and S. Lee. "Cross-Cultural Differences in Belonging and Psychological Safety: Evidence from Multinational Organizations." *Diversity & Inclusion Quarterly* 14, no. 2 (2025): 41–62.

Results Washington. "Crisis Communication: Leadership Steps for Transparency and Accountability." 2019. https://results.wa.gov/.

Rock, D. "SCARF: A Brain-Based Model for Collaborating with and Influencing Others." *NeuroLeadership Journal* 1 (2008): 44–52.

Rosso, B. D., K. H. Dekas, and A. Wrzesniewski. "On the Meaning of Work: A Theoretical Integration and Review." *Research in Organizational Behavior* 30 (2010): 91–127. https://doi.org/10.1016/j.riob.2010.09.001.

Sage Journals. "Predictive Validity of Belonging Measures in Organizational Settings." *Industrial and Organizational Psychology Quarterly* 47, no. 2 (2024): 156–171.

Schaufeli, W. B., A. B. Bakker, and W. Van Rhenen. "How Changes in Job Demands and Resources Predict Burnout, Work Engagement, and Sickness Absenteeism." *Journal of Organizational Behavior* 44, no. 8 (2023): 672–689.

Schein, E. H. *Organizational Culture and Leadership.* Jossey-Bass, 1985.

Seramount. *Measuring Belonging in the Workplace: Tools and Tactics to Create an Inclusive Workplace.* Seramount, 2024.

Shah, S. U. R., N. Sudibjo, K. Priyank, and H. F. A. Hasan. "Integrating Sustainable Human Resource Management: Review and Research Agenda." *Journal of Human Resource and Sustainability Studies* 11, no. 4 (2023): 210–232. https://www.scirp.org/journal/jhrss.

Shore, L. M., A. E. Randel, B. G. Chung, M. A. Dean, K. Holcombe Ehrhart, and G. Singh. "Inclusion and Diversity in Work Groups: A Review and Model for Future Research." *Journal of Management* 37, no. 4 (2011): 1262–1289. https://doi.org/10.1177/0149206310385943.

Simpson, R., and P. Lewis. "Bubbles of Belonging at Work: Redrawing Boundaries of Inclusion and Exclusion in a Changing Labor Market." *Work, Employment and Society* 39, no. 5 (2025): 841–860. https://doi.org/10.1177/09500170251350063.

Snijders, T. A. B., and R. J. Bosker. *Multilevel Analysis: An Introduction to Basic and Advanced Multilevel Modeling.* 2nd ed. Sage, 2012.

Sutcliffe, K. M., and T. J. Vogus. "Organizing for Resilience." In *Positive Organizational Scholarship*, edited by K. S. Cameron, J. E. Dutton, and R. E. Quinn, 94–110. Berrett-Koehler, 2003.

Tajfel, H., and J. C. Turner. "An Integrative Theory of Intergroup Conflict." In *The Social Psychology of Intergroup Relations*, edited by W. G. Austin and S. Worchel, 33–47. Brooks/Cole, 1979.

Temkin, B. "It's Time to (Re)Build Trust." *Humanity at Scale*, April 14, 2024. https://humanityatscale.substack.com/p/its-time-to-rebuild-trust.

Trivers, R. L. "The Evolution of Reciprocal Altruism." *Quarterly Review of Biology* 46, no. 1 (1971): 35–57. https://doi.org/10.1086/406755.

Twenge, J. M. *Generation Me: Why Today's Young Americans Are More Confident, Assertive, Entitled—and More Miserable than Ever Before*. Atria, 2010.

University of Queensland. *Leadership for Uncertain Times: Building Trust and Resilience in Organizations*. Brisbane, Australia: University of Queensland Business School, 2019.

"Various Articles on Ethics, Belonging, and Cognitive Dissonance in Organizational Change." *Journal of Business Ethics* 189, no. 4 (2024).

Visier. *Workforce Intelligence Report: The Cost of Turnover*. Visier Analytics, 2023.

Washington, E. "The Five Stages of DEI Maturity." *Harvard Business Review*, October 31, 2022. https://hbr.org/2022/11/the-five-stages-of-dei-maturity.

Washington State Auditor's Office. *Assessing Workplace Culture at the Department of Fish and Wildlife: Executive Summary and Audit Report*. Olympia, WA: Office of the Washington State Auditor, 2019. https://sao.wa.gov/sites/default/files/audit_reports/PA_DFW_Workplace_Culture_ar-1028973.pdf.

Weick, K. E. "Small Wins: Redefining the Scale of Social Problems." *American Psychologist* 39, no. 1 (1984): 40–49. https://doi.org/10.1037/0003-066X.39.1.40.

Wilson, D. S., and E. O. Wilson. "Rethinking the Theoretical Foundation of Sociobiology." *Quarterly Review of Biology* 82, no. 4 (2007): 327–348. https://doi.org/10.1086/522809.

Your Thought Partner. *Trust as Strategic Infrastructure: Board Oversight for ESG, DEI, and Belonging.* 2023. https://yourthoughtpartner.com/

Zak, P. J. "The Neuroscience of Trust." *Harvard Business Review*, 2017.

Additional Resources

The Glossary, FAQs, and Appendices are available digitally via the QR code. This format enables ongoing updates and additions, providing access to the most current tools, diagnostic templates, implementation guides, and reference materials as the work evolves.

Acknowledgments

Mentors and Minds

Mark Knauf, my brother, who nudged me beyond a maturity model to the standard itself. Your insight transformed this work from framework to foundation. You inspire me.

Mike Naylor, former President of Operations at Rubbermaid and former EVP of Strategic Planning at General Motors, you taught me the fundamentals of strategic planning that undergird everything in this book.

Sarika Garg (founder of CacheFlow, now part of HubSpot), when you joined Ariba, I had no clue how your work, values, and leadership would influence me. Sarika recruited me for Tradeshift. Your understanding of products and SaaS has expanded my perspective and fueled the potential of this work beyond words on a page.

Doug Folden (Partner at a16z, formerly Tradeshift, Malwarebytes, Ariba, Apple), the balance between "mind" and "leaders who shaped my understanding," and "those who carried the weight." Your perspective on leadership, management, and being human is baked into this book.

Craig Fisher, "let me introduce you to someone who made my books possible . . . Kory." As a kindred spirit, you provided hope.

Nicole Eisdorfer, a like-minded fellow traveller. Your feedback and insights came at the right time, allowing me to maintain faith in my work.

Bill Jensen, you were the first to consider the work that I've done as disruptive (in all the right ways). That moniker is something I've sought to live up to. I believe this might have done the trick.

Meg Bear, if not for you, I would have published a very different book. Your statement that this work is what is needed now spurred me to publish this book.

Leaders Who Shaped My Understanding

Derek Beckman, Jesper Helt, and John Lehockey—the good bosses who demonstrated that leadership and belonging aren't contradictory but complementary.

Family

Mary, Anna, and Ali—who remind me daily that belonging starts at home and extends everywhere we go. You provide perspective on what matters most.

Jim and Phyllis Knauf—for creating the foundation of belonging that made everything else possible. This work would not have come to life without you.

Acknowledgments

Colleagues Who Made It Real

Pernille Hippe Brun, Bryan Chaney, Hao Ming, Joe Illvento, Carmen Scanlon, Lydia Gee, Melissa Estrada, and Martin Rosengaard—who helped transform theory into practice and showed me what belonging infrastructure looks like when it works.

Those Who Carried the Weight

Steve Rawlings, John Nicholas, and Marc Wenzel—your minds and hearts amplified and bolstered me. You three have provided inspiration, reality checks, humor, and sage counsel when I needed it the most.

Partners in Publishing

Purple Acorn and KORY KIRBY BOOKS—for believing in this work and helping bring it to life.

About the Author & BelongHQ™

Eric Knauf, Founder of BelongHQ, is a seasoned talent leader, strategic adviser, and author specializing in fostering belonging and driving organizational performance. With extensive experience in global talent acquisition, process transformation, and scaling high-growth companies, Eric has led talent functions at leading organizations such as SAP, Workrise, Commvault, and Tradeshift. In addition to enabling strategic and mindful growth, Eric's work emphasizes the power of belonging and connection and leveraging the disruptive power of humanity to create impactful workplace cultures.

BelongHQ equips companies with audits, dashboards, and maturity road maps that tie belonging to retention, innovation, and strategic agility.

Learn more or contact us:
- www.BelongHQ.com
- info@belonghq.com
- LinkedIn: linkedin.com/in/eknauf

www.ingramcontent.com/pod-product-compliance
Lightning Source LLC
Chambersburg PA
CBHW060452030426
42337CB00015B/1556